"There is not a more pow＿ ＿u.cᴍent to the human heart than this: *You are totally loved and fully accepted.* We long to hear this from our dads. We hope to hear this from our spouse. And, we want to say this to our children. Because of Jesus, God the Father says to us: 'You are totally loved and fully accepted.' If you want to grow in this truth and experience this reality, *The Reckless Love of God* is for you!"

—**Darrin Patrick,** lead pastor of The Journey
(St. Louis, MO), vice president of Acts 29,
and author of *The Dude's Guide to Manhood*

"I can't think of anyone better to write a book on the love of God than Alex Early. His joy-filled relationship with Jesus is contagious. I'm thrilled that he's captured some of his theology and heart in this soul-filling book. I will be recommending it to both the religious and the irreligious for years to come."

—**Tony Merida,** founding pastor of Imago Dei Church
(Raleigh, NC), associate professor of preaching
at Southeastern Baptist Seminary,
and author of *Ordinary*

"The reality that 'God is love' is too easily domesticated and kept at arm's length. In *The Reckless Love of God*, Alex relishes in the joy and adventure that takes place when the love of God takes possession of our hearts."

—**Justin S. Holcomb,** Episcopal priest, professor
of theology at Gordon-Conwell Theological Seminary,
and author of *On the Grace of God*

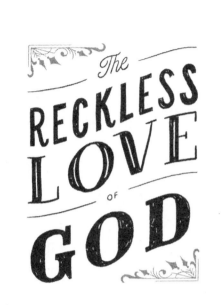

The

RECKLESS
LOVE
OF
GOD

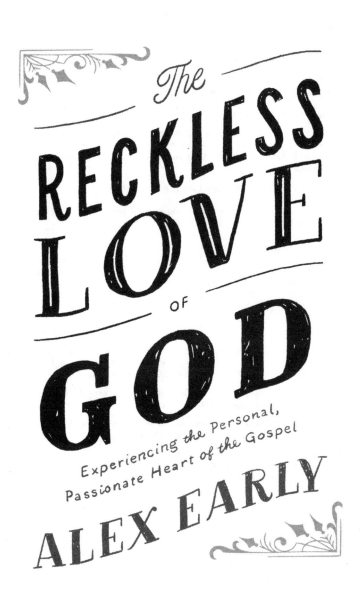

The
RECKLESS
LOVE
OF
GOD

*Experiencing the Personal,
Passionate Heart of the Gospel*

ALEX EARLY

BETHANYHOUSE

a division of Baker Publishing Group
Minneapolis, Minnesota

Published by Bethany House Publishers
11400 Hampshire Avenue South
Bloomington, Minnesota 55438
www.bethanyhouse.com

Bethany House Publishers is a division of
Baker Publishing Group, Grand Rapids, Michigan

Printed in the United States of America

                    Library of Congress Cataloging-in-Publication Data
Early, Alex.
    The reckless love of God : experiencing the personal, passionate heart of the
gospel / Alex Early.
        pages cm
    Includes bibliographical references.
    Summary: "Emphasizing that God's love isn't just a theological idea but a true, personal love that feels and even suffers, the author calls readers to consider the reality and significance of receiving this love"—Provided by publisher.
        ISBN 978-0-7642-1357-1 (pbk. : alk. paper)
    1. God (Christianity)—Love. I. Title.
BT140.E27 2015
231'.6—dc23   2015047388

In keeping with biblical principles of creation stewardship, Baker Publishing Group advocates the responsible use of our natural resources. As a member of the Green Press Initiative, our company uses recycled paper when possible. The text paper of this book is composed in part of post-consumer waste.

Cover design by Connie Gabbert

Author is represented by Wolgemuth and Associates.

15   16   17   18   19   20   21   7   6   5   4   3   2   1

green
press
INITIATIVE

I lovingly dedicate this book
to my absolutely stunning bride,
Jana
(my Yellowbird).

Contents

Introduction

"I hate that book."

This bold and angry statement came from a bold and angry young man. I said those words to my dear mother about nineteen years ago when I saw her Bible sitting on the passenger seat as I climbed into her minivan.

"Why does the Bible bother you so much?" she asked.

"I don't know. I just feel like every time I turn around, *God* is right there in my face. I can't get away with anything anymore! I wish he'd just leave me alone."

God, my soon to be Abba, was putting his heavy hand on me, and Jesus had his loving eyes on mine. I found I couldn't escape the Father's grasp or the Son's gaze. Maybe you know what I'm talking about. I assume if you've picked up a book called *The Reckless Love of God*, then you and I may have this experience in common.

Having been raised in a Christian home, I knew what God did for me through the cross of Jesus. I also knew that believing the Bible and embracing Jesus as my Lord and

Savior would permanently change everything about me. I was at a crossroads. I didn't like the idea of having a *Lord,* because it was too scary and too unpredictable to follow a God that I couldn't (and still can't!) physically see. I liked being in charge of my own little world. Being under someone else's authority did not sound appealing. Not one bit. Beyond that, I also had questions like, *Does God truly love me, or does he just want to tell me how to live my life? Where will this God take me? How will this God feel about me when I screw up? Will he want me even if I don't want him or forget about him? What will happen when we don't see eye to eye? Is he keeping score on me? If so, how will I know how I'm panning out?*

These questions kept me up at night.

Answers started rolling in on April 11, 1996. I heard a song that quoted John 3:16, a verse I'd heard my whole life, and yet right there, in rural Georgia (Butts County, to be precise), the Author of the Scriptures became the author of my salvation. I simply believed that "God so loved the world, that he gave his only Son, that whoever believes in him should not perish but have eternal life" (John 3:16). It wasn't evidence of God's existence I needed, but reassurance of his love for me.

So why do so many Christians need to hear this message of the reckless love of God again? The reasons are many. But one that stands out is that we are often way too satisfied with a study of God rather than an actual, intimate knowledge of him personally. As long as we can keep God as a subject to be examined under glass rather than a person to be encountered, we feel safe. "Doctrine is not a matter of talk but of life," John Calvin wrote. "It is not grasped by intellect alone, like other branches of learning. It is received only when it fills the soul and finds a home in the inmost recesses of the heart."[1]

We feel safer and in control with subjects. Relationships require so much more. Relationships speak of experience. And no, this is not an appeal to go on some sort of experience-driven, emotional roller coaster with God. However, to come in contact with the God of the universe and to be called his child is not dusty, old, impersonal theology. Theologian Paul Tillich says, "The courage to accept the forgiveness of sins, not as an abstract assertion but as the fundamental experience in the encounter with God,"[2] is what we are designed for. In fact, our feeling of safety is usually the first thing to go when we embrace vulnerability.

> **It wasn't evidence of God's existence I needed, but reassurance of his love for me.**

This reminds me of my sixth-grade dance. I took my friend Haley. We had known each other all our lives, starting as infants when our parents attended the same church. We went to preschool together and eventually all the way through high school. We had played in sandboxes and on playgrounds and had several birthday parties together. She was my buddy, and I knew taking her to the dance would be safe. However, when we got there we didn't dance, and it was my fault. Thanks to me, we stood across the cafeteria being completely awkward, both of us knowing that we should be acting silly, dancing, and enjoying ourselves, doing our best Michael Jackson moves. Haley wanted to dance. I think her friend even told me so. But I froze. I chickened out. I remember my neck and face turning red as I blushed at the thought of being seen "together" with Haley. For the first time in my life with her, I felt the pressure to betray who I was and exchange my authentic self for the awkward feelings that accompany preadolescence.

This is how I think most Christians view the love of God. We are content to stand across the room, trying desperately not to make eye contact with the God who "wants to dance." We'd rather just blush and remain completely invulnerable— keeping to ourselves, our supposed dignity intact—meanwhile, cringing inside, longing to be our true selves.

In this book, I want to talk to people who are willing to bare their souls. People who might say something to this effect: "I'm a Christian. But, to be honest, God feels a million miles away, and my life is just busy, it's cluttered, and there are a few relationship issues I've got going on. I've got my doubts, and I've certainly broken some commandments that I know I'll have to answer for. More than that, I'm bored to tears in church, and I might not even be able to find my copy of the Bible right now, because it's been so long since I picked it up. My soul is tired, and I guess I'm just waiting to get to heaven to catch up with God and get some rest, if I even get in at this point. I know my heart is harder, more stubborn, and more twisted than I want to admit. My mind is blurry, my soul is parched, my sight is dim. But you asked me to be honest, and that's where I really am when it comes to me and God."

Maybe your heart has grown cold toward God's love due to any number of experiences. Maybe your heart never really warmed up to his love to begin with. You are like many others in churches everywhere today. You may think that "Jesus Loves Me" is a nice song for children in Sunday school, but the reality of who Jesus is—that God's love isn't just for the world or the church but for *you* as an individual—that sounds like an overstatement. Thinking about an up close and personal experience of God's love simply doesn't move you. Or maybe you don't believe it. You've read the Old Testament. "I know how God *feels* about me," you say. "He's angry. He's always angry." Or maybe the thought of God's love scares you because you've seen or heard something that freaked you out a little. Maybe you were burned by a pastor or someone else in the church. Maybe a verse in the Bible offended you somewhere along the way. Maybe you question if Jesus is going to make your life even messier. (He certainly will in some ways.)

If that's you, I have news for you. Good news. As a human being, you are an image-bearer of God. And, as a Christian, even a rickety one, you are not just part of creation in general. You are a new creation (2 Corinthians 5:17) *and* God considers you to be one of his children (Romans 8:15; Galatians 4:6). That's right. You are in his family, and the Bible doesn't mince words when it comes to just how much God cares about his family.

Who This Book Is For

This is a book for those who have been crushed by the weight of legalism. For those who have tried and tried to earn the favor of God by relentless church attendance, diligent Bible studies, unbroken prayer, and tithing.

This is a book for those who have been content to warm themselves by the fire of God's love but never had the faith (or nerve) to actually step into the fire and be utterly consumed.

This is a book for those who think "Jesus Loves Me" is elementary. You have "graduated on" to more robust theological, philosophical, sociological, psychological, and anthropological endeavors. You may have been to seminary. Yes, my friend, this is for you too.

This is a book for those who get baptized or "go forward" every two or three years in order to secure their salvation because, obviously, it didn't "take" the last time.

This is for those who leave their Bible in the back of their car all week long, closed up in the sun.

This is for those who think they've gone too far and committed the "unpardonable sin," whatever that may be. The guilt-ridden and the shamed who think they've tapped out all of God's grace and find it amazing that he let them get this far.

This is for the promiscuous, the vagabond, the throwaway, the not good enough, the overachiever, the proud, the insolent, the angry, the forgotten, the brokenhearted.

This is also for those who find themselves safe in the arms of Abba and walking closely with Christ, loving his Word, empowered by the Spirit, and obeying his commands.

This is for the busy professor, student, stay-at-home mom, or workaholic. The gospel is for the tired preacher and even more tired preacher's kid. This is for the cage fighters, gamers, and athletes. This is for the Christian who knows Jesus as Lord, King, and Christ but hasn't dared to accept his brotherhood or enter into embracing his most endearing term for us: the *beloved* of God. This is for those who have become too familiar with God and have lost any sort of reverence before him. This is for those who call God Creator but not *Abba.* Maybe you're like me, and that word either keeps you guessing or makes you blush.

This is for those who have relegated and confined God to the outskirts of your mind and have opted to converse with him when convenient, on holidays, or when the unexpected tragedy strikes.

This is for black people, white people, brown people, yellow, red, purple (Tovah, my daughter, wishes everyone was purple), or any other people, all of whom are made in God's image. This is for the rich. This is for the poor. This is for the middle class. This is for men. This is for women. This is for homosexuals. This is for heterosexual perverts. This is for the friendless. This is for the divorced. This is for the addict. This is for the cheater. This is for the drunk. This is for the high. This is for the drug dealer. This is for the image-obsessed. This is even for those who don't finish these few short chapters.

The only way into Jesus' choir is to sing off-key. The only way into God's family is to own the fact that you don't deserve to be in it. The only way to abide in the presence of the Holy Spirit is to accept that you are accepted.

This is the gospel.

The Gospel

The good news is that God loves us *before* we become Christians. Our sins were placed on Jesus at the cross, and through his death and resurrection, he gifts us with his righteousness so that you and I, by God's grace, belong in the presence of God himself. That's right. You belong with God. And when you accept Jesus as your Savior, in God's eyes you have his reputation—totally blameless, totally righteous. You so belong with God that upon experiencing his reckless love for you as a person, it won't be long before you start thinking, *We were always meant to be together.*

Over the last decade or so, I have been thrilled to see—and be deeply changed and challenged by—the emphasis placed on the gospel by so many incredible Christian leaders. I grew up in a great church, a church that boldly preached the gospel of Jesus. Yet I don't remember hearing the word *gospel* buzz like it does today, and for that progress, I am very grateful. We are certainly living in a special time.

Hundreds of books and articles have been published by gifted pastors and authors, including *The Explicit Gospel* by Matt Chandler, *What Is the Gospel?* by Don Carson, and *Gospel* by J. D. Greear and Tim Keller. A *Gospel Transformation Bible* is even now available. Gospel-centered conferences, websites, and resources serve the church in tremendous ways. Beyond that, seeing brilliant minds unpack and expound on the gospel, and hearing how they go about articulating the good news, is fascinating. Trevin Wax has been compiling a document that is now up to thirty-one pages of definitions of *the gospel* provided by over fifty different theologians, historians, and pastors, each of which nuance different aspects of the good news.[3] Indeed, knowledge of *what* the gospel actually is these days is of utmost importance. Paul himself tells us that it is of "first importance" (1 Corinthians 15:1–3).

But Calvin admonishes us all not just to "talk about the Gospel, when it ought to reach and affect the inner longings of the heart. It should take possession of the soul and influence the whole personality a hundred times more than the sterile discussions of philosophers!"[4]

Many Christians gravitate toward the "what" of the gospel without considering the "*why*" that produced the "what." Knowing *what* something is is one thing; knowing the *why* that gave rise to the *what* literally changes everything. Why did God send Jesus? Further, why was Jesus willing to come for us? Why is there a rescue mission for rebels? Why would a king lay aside his heavenly crown for a crown of thorns? Why do we even have the opportunity to talk about this outrageous act of scandalous grace that has turned the world upside down? Here's why: the incredible love of God.

Many Christians gravitate toward the "what" of the gospel without considering the "why."

Within the Trinity exists perfect, eternal, radiant love. Just before Judas led the mob to Jesus in the garden of Gethsemane, Jesus was praying to his loving Father in heaven. Through sweat and blood, he said, "You loved me before the foundation of the world" (John 17:24). If perfect love were ever to exist, it would exist within the untarnished, completely sinless Holy Trinity. Later, the apostle John writes to the church in Ephesus:

> Beloved, let us love one another, for love is from God, and whoever loves has been born of God and knows God. Anyone who does not love does not know God, because God is love. In this the love of God was made manifest among us, that God sent his only Son into the world, so that we might live through him. In this is love, not that we have loved God but that he loved us and sent his Son to be the propitiation for our sins.
>
> 1 John 4:7–10

God *is* love. It must be understood that when we say God is love, love is not the only attribute he possesses. He exercises wrath, justice, righteousness, and many other attributes perfectly at all times. We must also remember that John's declaration that "God is love" is very different from saying "love is God." John, the disciple Jesus loved, makes it clear that everything God does comes from his heart of love.

Does God Actually "Feel" Things?

For some, it's hard to believe that God has actual feelings. You may think he's too big and too busy to feel something about little creatures like us. Historically, some Christian theologians have pushed back on this idea of God experiencing feelings as well, for if God were to experience feelings, he would be responding to his creation and thus be in a constant state of change; he would be merely reactionary. Therefore, they say, God cannot experience emotions because God cannot change. Change in God would imply there is weakness in God, and that simply cannot be. This idea bumps up against a long-settled doctrine known as the "impassibility of God," meaning that God is unchangeable. But to be clear, the doctrine of impassibility emphasizes the fact that God is not experiencing *involuntary* emotions and that he is constantly reacting to the world.[5]

There is nothing involuntary about God. Everything, literally everything, he does is eternal and for his own glory. This includes what we know of him internally and what we see of him externally. God is capable of feeling all sorts of emotions simultaneously about an infinite number of scenarios because he is God. He is what the famous twelfth-century

Italian priest and philosopher Thomas Aquinas said of him: God is *actus purus*—he is a "pure act."

In the Bible, from cover to cover, we see the writers of Scripture using language described by theologians with a "fifty-cent word"—*anthropomorphic*—when talking about God. That is to say, they assign humanlike traits to God. God can see, hear, grieve, rejoice, and sing. To say that God *doesn't* experience emotion in the name of preserving himself from weakness and suffering actually makes him appear weaker, not stronger. For as soon as we speak of love, we must speak of suffering, for they go hand in hand.

God is capable of feeling all sorts of emotions simultaneously about an infinite number of scenarios because he is God.

Here's what I mean. The German theologian Jürgen Moltmann, commenting on Fyodor Dostoevsky's *The Demons*, states that "a God who cannot suffer is poorer than any man. A God who is incapable of suffering is a being who cannot be involved. He cannot weep for he has no tears."[6] Or as the great philosopher from Notre Dame, Alvin Plantinga, says, "Some theologians believe that God cannot suffer. I believe they are wrong. God's capacity for suffering, I believe, is proportional to his greatness; it exceeds our capacity for suffering in the same measure as his capacity for knowledge exceeds ours. . . . So we don't know why God permits evil; we do know, however, that he was prepared to suffer on our behalf, to accept suffering of which we can form no conception."[7]

Do you see what Moltmann and Plantinga are getting at here? Love, tears, compassion, suffering, and real involvement in our world demand *real* emotions. God is not a cold, impersonal, disengaged, passive robot in the sky pretending to have emotions. Detaching oneself emotionally does not speak of love or even maturity. Unhealthy detachment smacks of self-preservation, refusal to be vulnerable, even narcissism. Though in debt to no man, God is a warm, loving Father who actually has emotions, though perfect in his expression of them at all times.

Let me show you three passages of Scripture from the Old Testament that capture exactly how God feels about his rebellious, selfish, wayward children. I have purposely turned to the Old Testament, because many are under the impression that the God of the Old Testament was mean, ruthless, and bloodthirsty. And the New Testament, as the consensus goes, records how God had a "change of heart" somewhere in that quirky intertestamental period and started to hand out kindness, grace, and love. Nothing could be further from the truth. As theologian Krish Kandiah points out, the idea that God started as a tyrant is longstanding, notably advanced in the second century by a bishop's son named Marcion:

> The Creator God of the Old Testament was obsessed with the law and was mostly angry and judgmental. Then there is a Second God, the good, gracious Father of Jesus, unknown to us before the New Testament. . . . Marcion was denounced as a heretic . . . but many Christians live as if Marcion was right.[8]

In the Old Testament, the people of God are referred to as *Israel* (which means "he struggles with God") or *Ephraim* (which means "fruitful"). Let's look at how tender our heavenly Father's heart is toward his children.

The Nursing Child

In Isaiah, God asks a rhetorical question and follows it with a powerful declaration:

> Can a woman forget her nursing child, that she should have no compassion on the son of her womb? Even these may forget, yet I will not forget you. Behold, I have engraved you on the palms of my hands.
>
> Isaiah 49:15–16

This isn't flowery rhetoric. God is speaking of the most intimate, vulnerable experience humans share, and that is a mother and her nursing baby. Not only would the mother not neglect her baby, but God says, "I have engraved you on the palms of my hands." Meaning, "See, you are in my hands. You are on me and I am holding you." In this image, the hands of God are open to his children, not close-fisted. They are welcoming, not scary. They are stretched out, ready to receive, not arms crossed, folded under his coat. He wants his little ones close to him.

The hands of God are open to his children, not close-fisted.

Learning to Walk

In Hosea, God says:

> When Israel was a child, I loved him, and out of Egypt I called my son. The more they were called, the more they went away; they kept sacrificing to the Baals and burning offerings

to idols. Yet it was I who taught Ephraim to walk; I took them up by their arms, but they did not know that I healed them. I led them with cords of kindness, with the bands of love. . . . How can I give you up, O Ephraim? . . . My heart recoils within me; my compassion grows warm and tender.

Hosea 11:1–4, 8

Again, God says explicitly that he loves his children. Just as I don't wait for my four-year-old son, Jude, to clean himself up before I will embrace him, so it is with God and his children. God doesn't wait around for his children to get their acts together and say they're sorry before he accepts them and extends love and forgiveness. On the days when we rebel against God, he isn't planning our demise. Far from it. While in our sin, at our darkest, God is thinking, *Oh, how I love my children. I can't give up on them.*

The Rebellious Child

In the eighth century BC, God's children were going astray after false gods and religions, and in complete rebellion against him. What did this stir up in God? Not resentment. Memories. As the passage from Hosea 11 shows, God shares memories of pure joy and tenderness. This isn't because God doesn't take sin and rebellion against him seriously. He does, as we will see. But first and foremost, his disposition is one of completely connected, deeply involved, incomprehensible paternal love.

The average child transitions from crawling to attempting his first steps around his first birthday, and babies learn to do this with the assistance of their parent. God, in this moment, says in effect, "I remember holding your soft little hands in mine. Your whole hands wrapped around my fingers as I held you up and helped you take your wobbly first steps." If you are a parent, you know this pulls at your heart, and that is precisely why God said it, because he actually *felt* and *feels* this way about his children, even on their worst day. This is not manipulation. This is not emotionalism. This is God's "alluring" us (Hosea 2:14). This is the Word of God from the mouth of the prophets.

Then, in Jeremiah, God gives us another set of rhetorical questions:

> Is Ephraim my dear son? Is he my darling child? For as often as I speak against him, I do remember him still. Therefore my heart yearns for him; I will surely have mercy on him, declares the LORD.
>
> Jeremiah 31:20

This is not the language of an employer-employee contract. Ephraim does not sound like a hired hand. No, this is God's covenantal love as an adoptive Father. God's heart is a yearning heart. God's heart is a feeling heart. God's heart is an active heart. God's heart is an attentive heart. God's heart is an intentional heart. The Hebrew word for "yearns" is *hama,* pronounced "hay-ma." According to scholars, "It is a strong word, emphasizing unrest, commotion, strong feeling, or noise."⁹ God has no children that he is not deeply fond of! He refers to each one of us as his "dear son," his "darling child."

God, through the timeless pages of the Bible, isn't mumbling in his irrevocable declaration of love for people like you and me. For sixty-six books, God has a consistent theme and he lifts his voice with a bravado that has shaken the earth to its core—a booming pronouncement that he, the very origin and definition of love, has his eyes fixed on *you*. And he goes beyond lifting his voice. God has given you a demonstration—a demonstration of just how much he loves you. God is not content to only feel and say that he loves us. He must show us his love specifically in his Son's death while we were still sinners (Romans 5:8). While meditating on the cross of Jesus, "Recognize the transcendent goodness of God . . . and his overflowing, superabundant love for man. Before such goodness and love nature trembles, sages stammer like fools, and the saints and angels are blinded with glory. So overwhelming is this revelation of God's nature that if his power did not sustain them I dare not think what might happen."[10]

> **God not only tolerates you and me, he actually likes us.**

Yes, God not only tolerates you and me, he actually likes us. What makes God love us like this? Is it because he sees something great, bold, heroic, or charming that he can't resist? Was it that charitable donation you made to a nonprofit last December? "What made him look my way?" you ask. The Bible uses a word for this kind of unearned affection: *grace*.

Our good works didn't get God's attention. Rather, our good works apart from God repulse him. God did not peer through the corridors of time and find you on your best day and think, *That one. She's for me! I can really use her for my glory! She and I will make a great team!* Martin Luther said, "It is a horrible blasphemy to imagine that there is any work whereby thou shouldst presume to pacify God, since thou seest that there is nothing which is able to pacify Him but this inestimable price, even the death and blood of the Son of God, one drop of which is more precious than the whole world."[11] No, he saw you on your worst day, filled with sinful thoughts, motives, intentions, and actions, and in that moment, in your darkest, most rebellious state, he loved you with a love that is otherworldly, literally, as John puts it, "from another country" (1 John 3:1, my translation).

In love, God gave his Son, Jesus, to die in our place as a substitute for all of our sins. He rose three days later and now sits as the ascended King of kings and Lord of lords. He is currently preparing a home for you (John 14:1–4), praying for you (Hebrew 7:25; Romans 8:34; 1 John 2:1), and is coming soon for you. In the Old Testament, your name was engraved on his hands metaphorically. In the New Testament, your name was engraved on his hands literally through Jesus' cross because God has always wanted you, Jesus loves you, and the Holy Spirit is drawing you, even now.

—— 1 ——

Jesus Loves Me
This I Know,
for the Bible Tells Me So

"When Christ speaks, it is God who speaks. . . .
The words of Christ are God's words. The actions
of Christ are God's actions. The human response
to Christ is the response to God."[1]

—Robert Kysar

I had just graduated with a BA in theology. Needless to say, I felt pretty confident, maybe too confident, in what I believed as a young Christian. Such enthusiasm often accompanies young theology students. Then one morning I read several passages in the New Testament that said Jesus made the world. How, I wondered, did these claims coincide with what is stated on the opening page of Genesis, namely that God made the world?

Here I was, with my new degree, asking, "Uh, who made the world?"

I had just spent four years studying the Bible, and I hadn't even thought to ask this basic question! Had I never looked around at the lakes, rivers, trees, stars, mountains, deserts, plants, and animals, and thought how all this beautiful, intricately designed world got here? On a smaller yet no less amazing scale, how did I not wonder who was responsible for making a tadpole develop into a frog? Did I not pay *any* attention in my systematic theology classes? Apparently not on the day we covered this crucial topic.

> Here I was, with my new degree, asking, "Uh, who made the world?"

With these seemingly contradictory God made the world/Jesus made the world passages in mind, I climbed into my dump truck and headed to work as a landscaper, my day job at the time. On this particular day, my boss called on my radio and said, "Hey, you're going to the home of a guy named Craig. He's a philosopher or something. You'll probably like him."

A few hours later I arrived at the job site and began to work on the homeowner's backyard. Soon, one of the top Christian philosophers and apologists in the world walked up to me wearing a Marist sweatshirt over a collared dress shirt, corduroy trousers, and boat shoes: Dr. William Lane Craig.

As a theology major, I knew very well who Dr. Craig was. He had publicly debated the most famous atheists and agnostics of our day, including Richard Dawkins, Christopher Hitchens, and Sam Harris.

"How's it going?" he asked.

"All good at this end, sir."

Here was my chance.

"Dr. Craig, I know you're at home, and you don't know me, and certainly, you don't have to talk with me, but I was just wondering if I could ask you one question."

Kindly, he replied, "That'd be quite all right. Ask away."

Covered head to toe in Georgia clay, hands cracked and scraped up, with dirt on my face and a hole in my steel-toed work boots, I asked, "Dr. Craig, who made the world?"

In his gentlemanly way, he replied, "Oh, that is a marvelous question. What makes you ask?"

"Well," I said, "I read my Bible this morning, and Genesis says God made it. Then, the New Testament seems to say Jesus made it. So, who made it? God or Jesus?"

Thoughtfully, Dr. Craig responded, "Maybe an illustration will help. Suppose I told you that I wrote a letter to Jones, my neighbor. Would you believe me?"

"Of course."

"What if I actually went inside, recorded the letter on my dictaphone, placed this on my secretary's desk, and she typed the letter and mailed it to Jones? Would you still say that I sent him a letter?"

"Yes, of course."

"Well," he continued, "that's what's going on in the Bible. Genesis is simply an abbreviated account of how the cosmos was made. The New Testament fills you in on the details of the 'secretary.'"

Problem solved! Sort of. Yes, God made the world. And Jesus also made the world. This makes sense. But it's one thing to realize who created the world. It's so much more to know that the Creator actually *loves* you.

Your faith will never be the same after experiencing the personal, passionate heart of the gospel.

Really, *Who* Is Jesus Christ?

Generations after the centurion in Mark's gospel confessed Jesus as God's Son, many of the world's "mighty" have wrestled with his greatness. The British socialist, historian, and novelist H. G. Wells (1866–1946) said, "I am an historian, I am not a believer, but I must confess as a historian this penniless preacher from Nazareth is irrevocably the very center of history. Jesus Christ is easily the most dominant figure in all history."[2]

Varied perceptions of Jesus' identity persist among Christian scholars, as well. Here, one encounters ideas that certainly don't square with those of Peter or even of Judas the betrayer. Noteworthy New Testament scholar Kevin Vanhoozer states:

> Whereas readers risk seeing themselves in the mirror of the text, historians are prone to see their own face at the bottom of a deep well and mistake it for the face of Jesus.[3]

The following is a sampling of the scholarly perspectives about Jesus today:

- An itinerate preacher
- A cynical sage

- The Essenes' righteous rabbi
- A Galilean holy man
- A revolutionary leader
- An apocalyptic preacher
- A proto-liberation theologian
- A trance-inducing mental healer
- An eschatological prophet
- An occult magician
- A Pharisee
- A rabbi seeking reform
- A Galilean charismatic
- A Hillelite or Essene
- A teacher of wisdom
- A miracle-working prophet and an exorcist[4]

In his classic *Mere Christianity*, Oxford don, literary scholar, and one of the most astute defenders of the Christian faith, C. S. Lewis, proposed the following argument regarding the nature of Jesus:

> I am trying here to prevent anyone saying the really foolish thing that people often say about Him [Jesus]: "I'm ready to accept Jesus as a great moral teacher, but I don't accept His claim to be God." That is the one thing we must not say. A man who said the sort of things Jesus said would not be a great moral teacher. He would either be a lunatic—on a level with the man who says he is a poached egg—or else he would be the Devil of Hell. You must make your choice. Either this man was, and is, the Son of God: or else a madman or something worse. You can shut Him up for a fool, you can

spit at Him and kill Him as a demon; or you can fall at His feet and call Him Lord and God. But let us not come with any patronizing nonsense about His being a great human teacher. He has not left that open to us. He did not intend to.[5]

Lewis (1898–1963) refused to acquiesce to those whose thinking was illogical and those who picked and chose their beliefs as they read Scripture. It's an all-or-none situation.

Can Matthew, Mark, Luke, and John Please Speak Up?

We can't help but breathe the air of doubt in this skeptical age in which people consume science fiction for entertainment and simultaneously strive to demythologize the Bible. Yet if we simply let the authors of the Gospels speak, we can figure out who Jesus is. Hans-Georg Gadamer was a nineteenth-century Bible scholar who specialized in hermeneutics, Scripture interpretation. He taught his students to understand that everyone brings pre-suppositions, histories, and attitudes to the ancient Scriptures. "Hermeneutics," he instructed, "is above all a practice in the art of understanding. . . . In it, what one has to exercise above all is the ear."[6]

If we simply let the authors of the Gospels speak, we can figure out who Jesus is.

In our culture today, we have confused hearing for *listening*. Hearing is done with zero intentionality. Listening actually requires paying attention to the one speaking. Contrary to what often passes for "historical biography"—poorly done documentaries streamed online—the gospel writers clearly state their views of Jesus' identity. In fact, the Bible argues that the Jesus of history is also the Christ of faith. The Bible declares that Jesus is the creator, sustainer, and ruler of the universe. Furthermore, he is coequal with God his Father. Jesus became man, lived a sinless life, died a sinner's death, was raised bodily from the grave, and triumphed over Satan, demons, death, hell, and the very wrath of God. He ascended back into heaven, is seated at the right hand of the Father, and will return to judge the living and the dead. Those who belong to him, by grace and through faith, will enter into eternal life in heaven. Those who do not will enter a place of eternal separation from God in a place that Jesus described as "hell."

Seeing that the Jesus who loves you and me is not only a good teacher, miracle worker, prophet, and good person, but is exactly what the Council of Nicea agreed him to be in AD 324—namely, "God from God, light from light, true God from true God"—should cause us to stand and marvel.

The unmovable mover and uncreated creator of the Greek Stoics, the eternal God of the Jews has accomplished something unique in the person and work of Jesus. No other world religion, philosopher, or politician matches his knowledge, power, authority, or love. In fact, every other religion in the world teaches that you must better yourself, pull yourself up by your own bootstraps, and then earn your keep in heaven by keeping the rules.

Jesus condescends to us and keeps the rules for us. His love is unconditional, his wisdom unsurpassed, his hope unrivaled, and his freedom unparalleled. All are available to you and me through entering a relationship with him. God almighty clothed himself in flesh and bones, entered our world, and relentlessly pursued us as disgruntled rebels. "God in Jesus became so much a part of a specific human context that many never even recognized that he had come from somewhere else," writes apologist and theologian Charles Kraft.[7] To the world, such is unabashed foolishness. To Christians, such is unspeakable joy and grace.

Jesus Christ Made Everything—Yes, Everything

Scripture repeatedly says that Jesus is not only God's Son, but that he is also the second person of the Trinity. This means that he is coequal and consubstantial (of the same essence) with God and is the co-creator of the universe. Please don't miss that last sentence. The Bible repeatedly emphasizes the fact that Jesus is God. He is not *a* god. He is not less than God. He is not created by God. He is not kind of *like* God. He is not just a good man. Jesus is the God-man. Jesus actually *is* God. This means that Jesus shares the glory of the one YHWH God on the first page of the Bible. *This matters immensely, for it is he who loves you.* The following Scripture passages illustrate these truths:

> In the beginning was the Word, and the Word was with God, and the Word was God. He was in the beginning with God. All things were made through him, and without him was not any thing made that was made. In him was life, and the life was the light of men.
>
> John 1:1–4

> Have this mind among yourselves, which is yours in Christ Jesus, who, though he was in the form of God, did not count equality with God a thing to be grasped, but emptied himself,

by taking the form of a servant, being born in the likeness of men. And being found in human form, he humbled himself by becoming obedient to the point of death, even death on a cross. Therefore God has highly exalted him and bestowed on him the name that is above every name, so that at the name of Jesus every knee should bow, in heaven and on earth and under the earth, and every tongue confess that Jesus Christ is Lord, to the glory of God the Father.

Philippians 2:5–11

He is the image of the invisible God, the firstborn of all creation. For by him all things were created, in heaven and on earth, visible and invisible, whether thrones or dominions or rulers or authorities—all things were created through him and for him. And he is before all things, and in him all things hold together. And he is the head of the body, the church. He is the beginning, the firstborn from the dead, that in everything he might be preeminent. For in him all the fullness of God was pleased to dwell, and through him to reconcile to himself all things, whether on earth or in heaven, making peace by the blood of his cross.

Colossians 1:15–20

Long ago, at many times and in many ways, God spoke to our fathers by the prophets, but in these last days he has spoken to us by his Son, whom he appointed the heir of all things, through whom also he created the world. He is the radiance of the glory of God and the exact imprint of his nature, and he upholds the universe by the word of his power. After making purification for sins, he sat down at the right hand of the Majesty on high.

Hebrews 1:1–3

When I saw him, I fell at his feet as though dead. But he laid his right hand on me, saying, "Fear not, I am the first and the last, and the living one. I died, and behold I am alive forevermore, and I have the keys of Death and Hades.

Revelation 1:17–18

The Holy Trinity—There's Only One . . . (or Three)!

In the third century, early church fathers wrote about the holy Trinity in the Athanasian Creed. Centuries later, this creed (belief) still explains what Christians mean by the word *God*: "Thus the Father is God, the Son is God, the Holy Spirit is God. Yet there are not three gods; there is but one God."

Three-in-one and one-in-three. It is simply stated, yet confounds minds around the globe. You may have heard various attempts to describe the Trinity: It's like a three-leaf clover; for example, it's one flower with three leaves. Or, it's like water, ice, and steam, all being the same element, but taking on different forms. Every metaphor used to describe the Trinity eventually breaks down. Why? Because there is no other *trinity* to which we can liken the Trinity. There's only one . . . or the three.

God's very being as the Trinity reveals much to us about himself—namely, that he is love. He is not only loving, but the definition of love. For if God were merely one, then he would have only himself at the center of himself, and that is what he calls "selfish." However, each member of the Trinity has the other two members at the very center of their being. They delight in one another. Jesus glorifies the Father (John 17:1), the Father glorifies Jesus (John 8:54), and the Spirit glorifies Jesus (John 16:13–14). It's a lot for us to process, but it means *the core of God's heart is love for Someone Else.* From there, that love within the Trinity spills over into the world and onto you and me.

Perhaps the most influential author I've ever read on this subject is Brennan Manning. The ragamuffin himself put it beautifully in *The Furious Longing of God*:

> The closer I come to death, the less inclined I am to limit the wisdom and infinity of God. The confession of John the apostle that *God is love* is the fundamental meaning of the holy and adorable Trinity. Put bluntly, God is sheer Being-in-love and *there was never a time when God was not love.* The foundation of the furious longing of God is the Father who is the originating Lover, the Son who is the full self-expression of that Love, and the Spirit who is the original and inexhaustible activity of that Love, drawing the created universe into itself.[8]

But how does God draw the created universe, including *you*, into himself? Through the incarnation—the clothing of God in flesh—the person and work of Jesus.

The Love of God Put On Display

I need to say it again: To comprehend God's love, we need to understand who Jesus is. And human attempts at articulating the identity of God simply will fall short. Not Abraham, Moses, Gandhi, Mother Teresa, Oprah, Dr. Phil, or even my Sunday school teacher can shed adequate light on the subject. Here's why: Human beings are riddled with flaws, mistakes, errors, and sin. No human being can show me God, much less God's perfect love. Even the prophets who wrote so beautifully about the love of God were sinners in need of the grace of God. Even the Israelites who journeyed with Moses in the desert could not grasp the fullness of God or the scandalous love in his heart. No, a much greater event than standing at the base of Mount Sinai was needed. God himself came down to this broken world, not shrouded in smoke and fire but in flesh and bone, to show us who he is and how he feels about us.

One barrier these days is that when people say the name *God*, they might be talking about different beings. Functional deists believe God made the world but that he's totally uninvolved, watching us from a distance. Who or what is God, exactly? Is God a he, she, it, them, they? Is God me, you, or us? Is God a cosmic power or an impersonal force? Without a name and a face, we are left to stare off into space, become stargazers, and discuss our finite speculations. Without tangibly seeing the love of God *demonstrated,* you and I are left to fill in the gaps about who God is and the nature of his love.

Questions about the identity of God are met with a clear answer and the objections to his love are dissolved in the person and work of his Son, Jesus. Thus, as Christians in pursuit of knowing and experiencing the personal love of God, we must go to the person in whom his love is most clearly expressed, Jesus.

When we consider God, we often think of the cosmos or the grandeur of creation. Yet planets, stars, solar systems, lakes, forests, mountains, seas, animals, and canyons cannot tell me just how much God loves me. Creation certainly causes my jaw to drop open in sheer awe, but in and of itself, that wonder cannot fill the black hole in my heart that is in desperate need of the love of God. Standing in awe of God's holiness, power, and majesty is one thing. Feeling loved by God as one of his children is quite another. As a person, a part of this creation, I'm limited in my capacity to know and *feel* loved. Thus, for God's love to be real to me, it must transcend impersonal created things and propositional truths, and become flesh and blood. My heart is too hard, my mind is too dull, and my soul too lost without a completely scandalous gospel.

In the passage quoted earlier in this chapter, the author of Hebrews tells us that Jesus "is the radiance of the glory of God and the exact imprint of his [God's] nature." Think about that for a moment. Jesus did not attempt to or hope to represent God. Jesus did not claim to be "a lot like God." Jesus did not merely function as a prophet and point people to God. Jesus is the *exact imprint* of God's nature. Thus, Jesus' claim to Philip at the Last Supper is stunning: "Whoever has seen me has seen the Father" (John 14:9).

> **Jesus did not merely function as a prophet and point people to God. Jesus is the exact imprint of God's nature.**

This means that how we see Jesus treating the tax collectors, the prostitutes, the broken, and the destitute is *exactly* how God feels about them and wants them treated. Jesus was also advocating for the poor, the broken, and the downtrodden when he got in the faces of the religious who wanted to reduce God to a mere cosmic vending machine that meted out punishment (blindness for the sinners as in John 9:1–12, stoning for the adulteress as in John 8:1–11, or grumpiness over healing on the Sabbath as in Luke 13:10–17). That the repeat offenders of the grace of God still needed another ounce of grace reveals the very heart of God. Why Jesus? Because the Bible goes beyond the speculative and the prophetic. Through Jesus, the author of Hebrews is saying that human speculation is met head-on in divine revelation. The mysterious identity of God is deciphered in the face of the Son. The timeless questions of the human soul, questions such as "Who am I? Why am I here? Where am I going?" are finally satisfied, not through ambition or fulfilling our dreams or becoming more successful, but in God's love made explicitly clear in the blazing heart and actions of his Son, Jesus Christ.

Before we voyage into the heart of the gospel—beyond human definitions and studies of God's love—I want to acknowledge that love, especially the love of God, can be difficult to embrace. Some people have been badly hurt by persons who proclaimed "love" for them. Others grew up in homes in which the word wasn't said much, if at all. You might be skeptical or afraid to enter into God's blazing heart for countless reasons. I understand. I have been there. With all this in mind, before you read further, I ask you to pause and pray this simple prayer:

God, here I am. I am going to say this as honestly as I can. I am a cluster of antonyms. I am bored, and overloaded with ideas. I believe in grace alone for salvation, but I work like I am still trying to earn

*your love. I believe I am your child, and yet I feel
like an employee. I am frustrated and yet totally
content. I am intelligent and yet so uninformed. I
have progressed but have hardly budged an inch. I
am creative, and yet influenced by others. I am eager
and reluctant. I am free and trapped. I weep with
John and your mother Mary, and still find time to
gamble at the foot of your cross. My honesty with
you sounds like insanity to me. Right now, help
me not to project my simple, limited, and deficient
understanding of what passes for love onto you.
These days, "love" is found on boxes of cheap
chocolates, in reality TV shows, and in the sewer
of porn. My culture repeatedly lies to me. I've told
many lies myself. So, would you project your love
onto me so that I can understand it and feel it?
Please speak freely and openly with me. I trust you.
Amen.*

2

Jesus **Loves** Me
This I Know,
for the Bible Tells Me So

"More pleasing to me than all your prayers, penances, and good works is that you would believe that I love you."

—Marjory Kempe of Lynn

A quick lesson in Greek: *Erythrophobia* is the fear of blushing. It comes from the Greek words for red and fear, and literally means "fear of redness." While I don't suffer from erythrophobia, I can't say that I enjoy the experience of blushing. The first time my wife told me she loved me, we were nineteen years old. I blushed! I tried not to, but I did. Hearing the word *love* just does something to us.

Yet, doesn't *love* remain the most overused, underfelt, and secularized word in the English language? I can easily move from saying "I love you" to my wife to "I love this steak" without blinking an eye. I know what I mean by the word in both contexts, and certainly my love for my wife supersedes my love for steak, no matter how fine the cut is. Still, for some, halfheartedly saying "God loves you" is as routine as "Good morning," or "How are you doing?"

Prominent thinker Aldous Huxley (1894–1963) wrote:

Of all the worn, smudged, dog-eared words in our vocabulary, "love" is surely the grubbiest, smelliest, slimiest. Bawled from a million pulpits, lasciviously crooned through hundreds of millions of loudspeakers, it has become an outrage to good taste and decent feeling, an obscenity which one hesitates to pronounce. And yet it has been pronounced, for, after all, love is the last word.[1]

With so many degrees of love, it's good to ask: Is God's love like my love? My parents' love? My spouse's love? Or does his love differ? Is it worth receiving? Does his love come with strings attached? Is it contractual or conditional? You know, the whole "I'll love you as long as you do _____ (fill in the blank) for me."

The Bible proclaims that Jesus' love qualitatively and quantitatively transcends any earthly love—whether from our spouse, our children, our parents, even love portrayed in the most sentimental movies. Conceptions of Jesus vary. Some view him as a far off, out-of-touch deity. Others regard him as a mystical, stoical philosopher, or as a good teacher who studies a lot but doesn't have much to say to regular folks. Still others classify him as a macho military general or mixed martial arts fighter who grounds and pummels weaker men.

Despite all the emotions and dispositions Jesus could have taken toward us, the Gospels convey his gripping, jaw-dropping, heart-stopping posture of love. In Matthew's gospel alone, Jesus uses the word *love* thirteen times. If, among his many other attributes, God is love (1 John 4:7), and Jesus is the image of God (Colossians 1:15) and the exact expression of God's nature and character (Hebrews 1:1–3), then all of Jesus' actions demonstrate love for God and others. But just who fits into this "others" category? Everyone. Yes, everyone. Whether religious or rebellious, Jesus came to demonstrate the kindness of God that leads us to repentance (Romans 2:4). Love for the least of these—the worst among us—the ones you and I would never expect, especially ourselves.

Is God's love like my love? My parents' love? My spouse's love? Or does his love differ?

The beloved apostle John wrote, "Children, our love must not be just words or mere talk but something active and genuine" (1 John 3:18 NJB). John certainly learned from Jesus' example. Yes, every act of Jesus recorded in the Gospels is an act of love. Every act. Each time Jesus, the Great Instructor, took the disciples, crowds, Pharisees, or even the "truth-seeking" Pilate to the School of God's Wisdom, Jesus' words flashed like lightning before them and, for a few, these words flashed *within*. Some merely *heard* Jesus and others *listened*. These flashing words conveyed love.

Jesus had plenty to say in the synagogues, on hillsides, and at meals with his friends who weren't "clean enough" to go to the synagogues because they were prostitutes or the types rejected from the local AA group for stubbornly deciding to keep messing up their lives. His patience didn't and doesn't run out when everyone else's does. His words differed from anything anyone had heard before. His words were of superior wisdom and unrivaled grace, words that exposed human frailties and removed the stains of past failures. His words destroyed and constructed, humbled and empowered. Words that lingered in the mind and kept one awake at night. Words of confrontation as well as consolation. Words that stung like a prophet, healed like a priest, and guided as a king. As *the* living Word, Jesus' words were consistently true.

Jesus never wrote a book. He spoke simply in parables. And from an initial, superficial reading of his teachings, one might mistakenly view him as superficial. This wasn't because he lacked information about anything in the galaxy! Surely, as God himself, he could have caused smoke to come out of people's ears as he explained how the Trinity works or some intricate eschatological nuance that many miss when they discuss the end of this age and the age to come. But he didn't do any of these "sensational" things. His sovereign hand rules, but his key concern is people's hearts and his key agenda is love to the glory of God.

Jesus, and those who were given ears to hear, heard from God's throne. The words, from the *Word* himself, illumined them. He was the light of man coming into the world (John 1:4). His words brought light to darkness— much like when Moses' face glowed before the burning bush. And just as Yahweh's words spoke of the liberation of his people, so too did Jesus' words. They still do, for he is the Son of God.

Jesus' sermons and conversations reveal not only God's mind but also his love. This love is not trite, generic, or commercial. Rather it is an uncomfortable, embarrassing, you-can't-be-serious kind of love. This love results in blushes even among the most confident.

God's love through his Son exceeded the descriptions given in Exodus, Jeremiah, Hosea, and other Old Testament books. Jesus descended; he became man to share God's love personally. Flesh and bone, hands and feet, eyes and ears, fingernails, eyelashes, blood, and sweat—all would be required to touch us.

Such touching comes with an enormous price. We are not God and cannot go to God regardless of how tall our towers might be or how good we think we are. Instead, *he must come* to us. He spilled an immense amount of blood, sweat, and tears to say, "I really know what you're going through. I can relate to you." Jesus comes to us face-to-face with honest eyes, open hands, and a willing heart to touch the deepest human wounds with the healing balm of God's presence. He did not remain transcendent; he became immanent. Fully acknowledging his equal status with God, he opened his hands and became man. Dietrich Bonhoeffer (1906–1945), from a Nazi prison camp, wrote,

> **Jesus comes to us face-to-face with honest eyes, open hands, and a willing heart to touch the deepest human wounds with the healing balm of God's presence.**

"It is only because he became like us that we can become like him."[2]

Scholar Matthew Elliott emphasizes the importance of Jesus' incarnation and the depths of his love, noting that "in the Gospels . . . we have found a Jesus who loves with a full and bursting heart. A Jesus whose great understanding of the character of God and understanding of men and women made in the image of God motivates a depth of love that cannot be contained but must be shared and expressed. This love, in turn, naturally motivates action(s)."[3]

Womb-Moving, Gut-Wrenching Compassion

In addition to demonstrating his superior authority, every miracle Jesus performed, whether restoring sight to the blind or feeding five thousand families, was his tangible way of saying, *"The fact that you suffer really matters to me, and I'm here to do something about it. My love has melted and become compassion toward you."* Yes, compassion! Disconnected systematic theologians who say that God lacks passion have neither closely read the Bible, nor have they allowed their Bibles to closely read them. Remember what Jesus said: "The Most High . . . is kind to the ungrateful and the evil" (Luke 6:35).

Personally and theologically speaking, one cannot talk about Jesus' love divorced from his *compassion*. Hebrew scholar Brad Young writes:

> The foundation of his [Jesus'] ministry was healing love for others. The sacrificial love of Jesus was deeply rooted in the Jewish understanding of divine compassion for people

created in the image of God. This love was not a formless love for humanity—it was a love *for the individuals that Jesus met.* Love saw *a person* who had great value in the mind of God, love had compassion for *a person* who has needs and struggles and took radical action on behalf of his neighbor.[4]

The Dialogue That Changed the World

God loving the world through Jesus is a familiar concept for many. In fact, the most popular verse in all of Scripture is undeniably John 3:16: "For God so loved the world, that he gave his only Son, that whoever believes in him should not perish but have eternal life." Today you'll see this verse on poster boards and held up in football field end zones, and, if not memorized, at least recognized by countless people who would not consider themselves Christians.

And yet, what gave rise to these famous words? What was the context in which they were originally said? Jesus said these words to an affluent Jewish man named Nicodemus. Nicodemus not only belonged to the religious party known as the Pharisees, he was a ruler in the separatist party (Pharisee literally means "separatist"). These devout men were known to have memorized most, if not all, of the Old Testament. Yes, the verses that we wrack our brains to understand, they memorized. The books in the Old Testament that take some Christians forever to find . . . *memorized.* They were a well-educated group, but more than that, they carried incredible political power.

The gospel of John tells us that Nicodemus went to Jesus in the middle of the night to talk. John doesn't tell us why he went in the middle of the night, so we can only speculate. Maybe Nicodemus was afraid to be seen by his peers speaking to such a rebel and outcast as Jesus was seen to be. Maybe it was the only convenient time to talk to Jesus. Maybe Jesus was so bombarded by people during the day that this was the only opportunity to grab a few moments with him and ask him the hard questions. We don't know. Two things stand out, however. First, Jesus didn't owe a conversation to Nicodemus or anyone else, but he obliged him. And second, Nicodemus had heard much about the works of Jesus and was convinced that God was with him (John 3:2). Thus, forgoing sleep to talk with Jesus won out that night for him.

Nicodemus went to Jesus and called him *Rabbi,* a term of honor and respect that means "teacher." The dialogue that followed changed the world. Jesus' teaching and power are acknowledged to be accompanied by God, but his first words to Nicodemus seem out of place or sudden. He simply says, "Unless one is born again he cannot see the kingdom of God." Nicodemus is puzzled, and they go back and forth about what Jesus means by being "born again." Jesus explains that to enter this world, all one needs to do is be born biologically through the labor of one's mother. This birth provides life for roughly eighty years (29,200 days). Similarly, one's spiritual *rebirth* is brought about by the labor of another: the Holy Spirit.

Here Jesus declares that any individual is capable of being born again. And those who are inherit *eternal* life at that very moment. The torch is lit, never to burn out or be extinguished. What man brings forth is susceptible to death and decay. What God brings forth is immortal.

Compassionate Love

In today's culture, as noted earlier, we cheapen deep words by their overuse, abuse, or misreading. *Compassion* tends to be one of those words. A study of the word *compassion* in many translations of the New Testament proves how limited English is compared with the original Greek. Jesus is described as being compassionate in our English translations, and the word's semantic range includes

"Having compassion" (ESV, NASB)

"Took pity" (NIV)

"His heart broke" (MESSAGE)

"Moved with pity" (WEYMOUTH)

"Felt sorry for them" (GW, NCV)[5]

In the *Tyndale Bible Dictionary,* W. A. Elwell and P. W. Comfort explain: "One of the Hebrew words translated 'compassion' is derived from a root word meaning 'womb,' thus comparing God's love with maternal love." Indeed, a mother feeling the flutter of her baby in the womb is said to be more bonding than possibly any experience in the world. That first flutter that grows into kicks and rolls across her belly cements a mother and child's souls together forever. This is getting at the essence of the word *covenant,* which is most often used in context with our most prized relationships.[6] A covenant is the opposite of a contract. Contractual relationships say, "I'm committed to these following things and no more." Moreover, a contract says, "If you fail to live up to any of these expectations, the contract is terminated." A covenant agreement says, "I am committed to *your good* no matter how many times you break my heart, and I will lovingly abide with you through my unmet expectations." That's God's heart toward his people.

Elwell and Comfort continue: "God's compassion, however, went beyond simply feeling the emotion; it was always demonstrated by definite acts that testified to his covenant with Israel."[7]

"I will lovingly abide with you through my unmet expectations." That's God's heart toward his people.

I have two children. My wife and other mothers have told me that no experience is more intimate, personal, hopeful, sacred, or holy than being a mother.

The Greek word for "compassion" is *splanchnizomai*. It comes from the word *splanchna*, meaning "bowels," "guts," or "entrails." It is interesting that in both the Hebrew Old Testament and the Greek New Testament, when it comes to speaking of compassion, the writers point not to their brains or their hearts but to their bellies. Here's why. The deepest parts of a human being are the sources of our most powerful emotions, such as the purest love and the deepest hatred.

Some think Jesus' compassion is only for the masses, others think small groups, and still others think it is only for individuals. The reality is that the Gospels actually give us all three scenarios and all use the word *compassion* to describe Jesus' feelings.

Compassion for the Crowds

In Mark 6:32, we read that Jesus and his disciples sought "a desolate place" where they could rest. (Matthew 14:15 tells the same story.) They were in a boat on the Sea of Galilee when a massive crowd spotted them and ran ahead to where they were going to dock. Before I continue telling the story, how do you think the disciples felt, having been so busy healing folks, preaching the gospel, counseling with people, praying over the sick, and feeling their own rumbling stomachs due to missing lunch? It isn't hard to imagine irritation, resentment, frustration, or even anger racing through a few of their minds. Maybe they began to grumble. Maybe not. One thing we know for sure is that when Jesus looked up and saw the crowd that numbered upwards of five thousand families, both Matthew and Mark said Jesus had compassion on them, "because they were like sheep without a shepherd" (Mark 6:34). The gut-wrenching compassionate love of God could not be hidden from his face. Following his heart (or guts), he healed the sick (Matthew 14:14) and fed their souls with the Word of God (Mark 6:34) and their stomachs with a single meal of bread and fish that was multiplied miraculously thousands of times over (Mark 6:41–42).

Compassion for the Few

Jesus' compassion goes beyond working miracles for crowds. In Matthew 20:29–34, the evangelist records the story of two blind men on the side of the road outside the town of Jericho. They had heard Jesus was merciful and could work miracles. They called out to him, "Lord, have mercy on us, Son of David!" The crowd rebuked the men, but they persisted all the more. They were in need, and Jesus was nearby. When Jesus stopped and asked what they wanted, they boldly asked for their sight to be restored. Neither under compulsion nor out of obligation, and certainly without attempting to wow the crowds, Jesus "had compassion on them and touched their eyes. Immediately they received their sight and followed him" (Matthew 20:34 NIV). Imagine being totally blind and the first face you see is God's Son, looking into your eyes, not with disgust, disdain, or disappointment but with compassion, love, joy, and acceptance.

Have you looked into his eyes lately?

Compassion for the One

So from crowds of thousands, down to a couple of men on the side of the road, Jesus is found expressing *compassion*. Permit me to take a little more space in sharing the story of an individual who experienced Jesus' great—some might say reckless—compassion and love.

The first chapter of Mark presents us with a man suffering from leprosy (vv. 40–45). Unlike today, in the first century leprosy could not be treated. Contracting this horrific skin disease resulted in multiple problems, including skin lesions, nerve issues, and deformities. It was not only physically devastating, but the carrier was bound to endure ostracism from society and even rejection from the religious community for being ceremonially "unclean." Moses prescribed quarantine in the law for the leper; they must be removed from the rest of society. Some Jewish teachers saw the disease as God's judgment on the leper's sin (usually slander).

In Leviticus 13, we read: "The leprous person who has the disease shall wear torn clothes and let the hair of his head hang loose, and he shall cover his upper lip and cry out, 'Unclean, unclean.' He shall remain unclean as long as he has the disease. He is unclean. He shall live alone. His dwelling shall be outside the camp" (Leviticus 13:45–46). The first-century Jewish historian Josephus speaks of the banishment of lepers as those "in no way differing from a corpse."[8] Many rabbis described lepers as "the living dead,"[9] whose cure was as unlikely as raising the dead. Some believed that even the shadow of a leper was contaminated.

Lepers were allowed the opportunity to go to synagogue to worship but would have to sit behind a screen, so as not to contaminate anyone else. The unclean watching the clean from behind a screen. If a leper entered a house, the house would be contaminated, or if he stood under a tree, those who would walk under that tree would be considered defiled. Leprosy went beyond a horrible illness. Leprosy sent the individual into severe isolation, a prison with no bars. The disease not only robbed the leper of his health, but his name, occupation, habits, family and friendships, and worshiping community.

Ignoring the requirement to keep fifty paces away from others, the leprous man recorded in Mark 1 approached Jesus and begged to be made clean. Undoubtedly the disease had stripped away the man's normal life. No family or friends around him for birthday celebrations or anniversaries. His uncleanness forbade him a brother's embrace, a kiss from his wife. He would never hold a daughter's hand or wrestle with a son.

"Moved with pity, he [Jesus] stretched out his hand and touched him and said to him, 'I will; be clean.' And immediately the leprosy left him, and he was made clean" (Mark 1:41–42). Jesus was moved from his innermost being, and his compassion manifested itself in the work of his hands, not just the words of his mouth. Jesus had to forgo his reputation in order to touch the living dead. He didn't care what others thought about him. He came to identify with those whom the religious crowd would not dream of touching. Jesus didn't have to touch him. He healed many people by simply speaking the word, and they were healed. *But he knew how important it was for this man to see Jesus reach out, transcend all cultural and social boundaries, and touch him in order to heal him.*

So what is Scripture saying about Jesus' love and compassion? When Jesus encounters those in society who are "quarantined" or pushed to the outskirts or ignored—the drunk, the prostitute, the addict, the throwaway, the repeat offender, the workaholic, the overachiever, the unemployed, the single mom, the businessman, the victim, the divorcee, the confused, the downtrodden—he radiates *splanchnizomai.* The empty-handed and brokenhearted are who Jesus came for.

When I say that Jesus loves you, know that when Jesus looks at you, both in your greatest strength and most profound weaknesses, his gut wrenches with love and his heart opens from the depths of his being. He *feels for you.*

Today, no matter where you are, what you've done, what's been done to you, what you're addicted to, simply close your eyes and picture Jesus of Nazareth, looking you in the face tenderly, filled with *splanchnizomai* for you. Princeton theologian of the nineteenth century B. B. Warfield wrote in a short essay, "He [Jesus] has not only saved us from the evils which oppress us; he has felt for and with us in our oppression, and under the impulse of these feelings he has wrought our redemption."[10] The French monk Brother Lawrence, whose seventeenth-century *The Practice of the Presence of God* remains a classic, once prayed, "O Lord, enlarge the chambers of my heart that I may find room for Thy love. Sustain me by Thy power, lest the fire of Thy love consume me."[11]

It is certainly one thing for Jesus to feel compassion toward the hungry, the downtrodden, and the broken. But what about the occasions in which he was in conflict with the Pharisees, or frustrated with the stubborn disciples, or simply angry? Did anything good come out of these scenarios? Was he filled with compassion in these moments too?

When Jesus looks at you, both in your greatest strength and most profound weaknesses, his gut wrenches with love.

Though Scripture doesn't explicitly say that Jesus felt *splanchnizomai* in heated moments, it is hard to look at the entire picture of how he is presented in the Gospels as being, and extending, anything other than love and compassion. Indeed, in Mark 3, Jesus healed a man's withered hand on the Sabbath day out of sheer "anger" (v. 5) toward the religious who would forbid such "work" on the Sabbath. Yes, he was angry with this hyper-religious crowd that desired to keep the Law perfectly. But Jesus appealed to the law of love and healed someone in need.

This is what righteous anger looks like. Seeing the injustice and commercialization of the worship of God at the temple, Jesus wove a whip (John 2:15) and drove out the money-changers so as to restore the temple to its rightful purpose— a place of prayer for the nations. It may not strike you as "loving" to see Jesus flipping tables and driving people out of the temple with a whip, but it was. How? He was loving the oppressed *and* the oppressor. The oppressed were being defended. The oppressor was being confronted. At the end of the day, to confront someone who is in sin is actually to love that person, not hurt him or her. Allowing someone to persist in their sin is the opposite of love. All that Jesus did was a demonstration of the perfect grace and truth of God (John 1:17).

Today, many are being way too soft on sin in the name of grace. The most dishonoring thing we can do to God is call good what he calls evil. The most graceless thing we can do to others is to leave them in their sin while we possess the keys of abundant life known as truth and repentance.

The Bells

One metaphor that may acquaint us with Jesus' loving, compassionate ministry is bells. In some traditions, at two of the most significant milestones of life—weddings and funerals—bells ring. On such occasions, bells mark beginnings and endings. They may also symbolize laughter and hope as well as mourning and questioning. It's no surprise that the gospel writers present our Lord Jesus at both weddings and funerals. We'll begin with a funeral.

Death Bells Toll

The investigative reporter Luke tells us of Jesus' compassion as he interrupted a funeral procession:

Soon afterward he went to a town called Nain, and his disciples and a great crowd went with him. As he drew near to the gate of the town, behold, a man who had died was being carried out, the only son of his mother, and she was a widow, and a considerable crowd from the town was with her. And when the Lord saw her, he had compassion on her and said to her, "Do not weep." Then he came up and touched the bier, and the bearers stood still. And he said, "Young man, I say to you, arise." And the dead man sat up and began to speak, and Jesus gave him to his mother. Fear seized them all, and they glorified God, saying, "A great prophet has arisen among us!" and "God has visited his people!" And this report about him spread through the whole of Judea and all the surrounding country.

Luke 7:11–17

As the woman of Nain followed her son's casket and the procession continued, Jesus stood in the crowd, neither distracted by the mundane nor aloof. We don't know Jesus' exact thoughts, but his compassion must have given rise to thoughts like *Who will care for this widow now that her husband and son are gone? She'll be alone, heartbroken, unsafe, vulnerable, angry, and confused. She'll spend her days outside my Father's house. The uptight religious crowd will probably judge her negatively, thinking, "Clearly, Yahweh is unhappy with you."* Such thoughts likely prompted Jesus' compassionate heart to defy convention, mercifully bow down, touch the dead son, and restore his life. This is reckless love.

Wedding Bells Ring

Moving from the historian doctor Luke to the beloved disciple John, we see another aspect of Jesus' compassion. In his gospel, John introduces Jesus differently than the other three gospel writers. He says that Jesus came to exegete the

Father—to reveal exactly what God is like (1:18). Such sets the stage for chapter 2 and Jesus at the wedding feast in Cana:

> On the third day there was a wedding at Cana in Galilee, and the mother of Jesus was there. Jesus also was invited to the wedding with his disciples. When the wine ran out, the mother of Jesus said to him, "They have no wine." And Jesus said to her, "Woman, what does this have to do with me? My hour has not yet come." His mother said to the servants, "Do whatever he tells you."
>
> Now there were six stone water jars there for the Jewish rites of purification, each holding twenty or thirty gallons. Jesus said to the servants, "Fill the jars with water." And they filled them up to the brim. And he said to them, "Now draw some out and take it to the master of the feast." So they took it. When the master of the feast tasted the water now become wine, and did not know where it came from (though the servants who had drawn the water knew), the master of the feast called the bridegroom and said to him, "Everyone serves the good wine first, and when people have drunk freely, then the poor wine. But you have kept the good wine until now." This, the first of his signs, Jesus did at Cana in Galilee, and manifested his glory. And his disciples believed in him.
>
> vv. 1–11

In first-century Palestine, men usually operated in the public spheres of business, commerce, and exchange. Women managed the private spheres, focusing primarily on aspects of the home, such as the kitchen and nursery.[12] This newly married, unnamed couple in Cana, who had been celebrating with friends and family, were about to experience public shame. In Palestine's honor/shame culture, this would have devastated this new family. At their wedding party, the good wine was served first, and as the week-long party continued, the cheap convenience store wine remained. Soon it was gone too; they had completely run out of this key part of the feast.

Working secretly, Mary, Jesus' mother, asked him to get involved and solve this huge dilemma. Initially, Jesus seemed to disrespect his mother by addressing her as *woman* and by appearing to be reluctant to help. But, Jesus wasn't dishonoring his mother at all. Rather, his focus remained on glorifying his Father, loving this couple, and sparing them from shame by turning at least 120 gallons of water into the finest port imaginable. The seventeenth-century English poet Richard Crashaw captured this when he wrote "The conscious water saw its God [Creator] and blushed."

Love does this.

3

Jesus Loves **Me** (Part 1) This I Know, for the Bible Tells Me So

"We cannot argue ourselves into knowledge of another person. That person must meet us, and we must learn by speech, action, event, to know that person in the concreteness and particularity of his person. The Christian testimony is that God has so acted, so spoken, so given himself to us in Jesus, that we know that he loves us, and that that knowledge is constantly confirmed and enriched through the events of daily life."[1]

—Lesslie Newbigin

Does anyone get uncomfortably close to you in conversation? Close talkers don't seem to realize how they intrude on our personal space. At times they can seem rude, or plain clueless.

You might be surprised that I see God as a close talker. But he lovingly invades our space so that we not only hear his words but *feel* his presence. It can feel uncomfortable, but he wants more than a passing "hello" from us in the hallway. He wants our love. Jesus loves the church, the family of God, so much that he "gave himself up for her" (Ephesians 5:25). And through his blood, we rebels can become the children of God and part of the body of Christ.

This is why I am so excited about the incredible amount of material being written and preached about church planting. I've given my life to the serving and planting of local churches. But can church life make it harder to believe that God loves us as individuals?

In countless conversations in recent years, people have consistently told me they believe God is loving, compassionate, caring, and forgiving when it comes to the world in general, the church at large, and other people. But they struggle to accept God's personal, passionate, transformative love for themselves as individuals. They find it easy to tell someone, "God loves you," but hard to say to their own soul, "The God of heaven and earth loves *you*."

Can church life make it harder to believe that God loves us as individuals?

Many things contribute to this struggle, but, like it or not, church dynamics may be at work. Many believers simply see themselves as nameless faces in the crowd—just like at a sporting event, a concert, or a citywide parade. They lose their sense of autonomy in the name of being a part of the group. *God loves this collection of people—this church,* they think. And it is true—God does love the church. (More on the church in the Conclusion.) However, when we look at the ministry of Jesus, one hardly gets the impression that he saw nameless faces in crowds. That is not the Jesus of the Bible. The Jesus revealed in Scripture sees people for the individuals they are, and he went out of his way to make people grasp this reality.

The Sermon on the Mount

The most famous sermon in the world, the Sermon on the Mount, was delivered by Jesus and recorded in the gospel of Matthew, chapters 5 through 7. Considered by some as *the* Christian ethic and also referred to as the "new law" for God's people, the sermon could have been a list of do's and don'ts or a tyrannical rant that sought to wield power over the people. The 111 verses could have been mere pontifications on who God is and what makes a Utopian society.

Instead, from what Jesus taught that day and *how* he taught it, the Sermon on the Mount reveals the love of God for people. Look at how Scripture sets the scene: "Seeing the crowds, he went up on the mountain, and when he sat down, his disciples came to him. And he opened his mouth and taught them" (Matthew 5:1–2).

Jesus saw the crowds and could have tried to dodge them. He could have opened with a scathing commentary on how awful they were in their sin. Instead, he simply took the posture of a traditional rabbi and sat down and taught the people.

Teaching is more than a job or a task. At its core, it is a labor of love. The very concept of teaching implies that one person has knowledge and another person is in need. It is not just as an impartation of data. It is a way to honor another human being. My mom and my brother are teachers—educators have a special place in my heart.

Consider the far-reaching care for us expressed in these four things that Jesus taught in the Sermon on the Mount.

First, Jesus gave us the famous Beatitudes, in which he explains clearly how we can live a life that is blessed by God. Such knowledge is undeserved.

Second, in chapter 6, verse 2, Jesus teaches that following and belonging to this great God of love will overflow in a life that looks for opportunities to help others in need. He doesn't say, "*If* you give to the needy," he says, "*When* you give to the needy," and he follows it by saying, "Sound no trumpet before you," meaning: Don't call attention to yourselves and seek applause for being the local humanitarian. As Paul says, "Let love be genuine" (Romans 12:9).

Third, Jesus knew the stresses and fears we face in this world, and taught his followers to "be anxious for nothing." We go through divorces, lose jobs, fall ill, and certainly we have all buried someone whom we deeply loved. Is the God of heaven really concerned about what worries us? Does he care about the debt that looms over our heads? Or health problems that make us think we'll never be well again?

The apostle Peter, who spent years with Jesus and was one of his closest disciples, later wrote, "Humble yourselves . . . casting all your anxieties on him [Jesus], because he cares for you" (1 Peter 5:6–7). Why would Peter say something like that? When problems arise, aren't we supposed to get tough, not moan about anything, and just press on in total victory? Not exactly. Jesus had borne Peter's burdens first-hand, and Peter boldly shares the message that Jesus is reliable—he can carry our load. Jesus is big enough to handle what keeps us up at night. He wants the weight on his shoulders, not ours. Jesus truly knew what he was getting when he bought us, and he bought us anyway—burdened, anxious, addicted, insecure, and afraid. He wants your burdens, and he wants *you.*

> **Jesus is big enough to handle what keeps us up at night.**

Last, consider that Jesus tells the crowds God is not some far-off, transcendent deity that doesn't desire communion with his creation. No, this view, deism, is the furthest thing from the truth. Jesus teaches that the crowds should relate to God as their Father—a Father who lovingly provides for those who ask, seek, and knock. God is not merely a force to be reckoned with or some cold statue. The true identity of God is a Father who is eager to provide for his children.

The Sermon on the Mount is an act of pure grace, not law. What frames the exhortations, rebukes, corrections, and admonitions is not merely rhetoric. Nor is Jesus simply making the Old Testament law harder by adding a few more rules. Instead, in love he is teaching God's image-bearers how to live. That's right. The lens God uses when he looks at you and me is love.

But not all were open to or welcomed Jesus' revelation of a no-strings-attached God. Jesus graciously accepted vagabonds, which prompted the religious scorekeepers to gnash their teeth at him. Luke records, "Now the tax collectors and sinners were all drawing near to hear him. And the Pharisees and the scribes grumbled, saying, 'This man receives sinners and eats with them. So he told them this parable . . .'" (Luke 15:1–3). That parable of the lost sheep, along with two others, shows just how potent, how scandalous, how vast the love of God is.

The Sheep, the Coin, and the Son

More than "receiving" tax collectors and other sinners, Jesus went so far as to eat meals and fellowship with those who were repulsive in the eyes of Jewish leaders. Company at the meal table was a massive cultural statement in the first-century Jewish community. Table fellowship was one way of practicing what they believed about God, themselves, and others. Ancient Jews believed in two altars. The first was the sacrificial altar in the tabernacle. The second was in the home. And this altar had a tablecloth.

Jesus was breaking their rules (again) by being *in the company* of his friends—"tax collectors and sinners"—when he told three unforgettable parables to the Pharisees and scribes.

> What man of you, having a hundred sheep, if he has lost one of them, does not leave the ninety-nine in the open country, and go after the one that is lost, until he finds it? And when he has found it, he lays it on his shoulders, rejoicing. And when he comes home, he calls together his friends and his neighbors, saying to them, "Rejoice with me, for I have found my sheep that was lost." Just so, I tell you, there will be more joy in heaven over one sinner who repents than over ninety-nine righteous persons who need no repentance.
>
> Luke 15:4–7

This parable reveals that the one wayward sheep deeply matters—the one that is "lost," the one that is alone, the one that is out in the open, subject to danger. The one sheep is actually worth pursuing. Why? To us, it's just a sheep. Yet the shepherd seems to take no thought of leaving the ninety-nine in order to rescue the one. And when he finds it, the sheep is not scolded, yelled at, or beaten. He picks it up, places it on his shoulders, and carries it back. The shepherd then throws a party and rejoices. Seems a bit extreme to throw a party over a sheep, doesn't it? Heaven remains fairly quiet over the ninety-nine rule keepers. Yet heaven erupts in celebration when one person owns his or her sin, sees the need of a savior, and cries out for grace. *That* kind of thing is what Jesus says causes heaven to throw a party.

There is more rejoicing in Jesus' next parable:

> Or what woman, having ten silver coins, if she loses one coin, does not light a lamp and sweep the house and seek diligently until she finds it? And when she has found it, she calls together her friends and neighbors, saying, "Rejoice with me, for I have found the coin that I had lost." Just so, I tell you, there is joy before the angels of God over one sinner who repents.
>
> Luke 15:8–10

In Bible times, a silver coin was worth approximately a day's wages. Could the woman survive without it? Probably. But she lights a lamp and frantically searches until, suddenly, there it is! The coin. And like the shepherd, she is filled to the brim with joy. Why? Because it is *her* coin.

> **Heaven erupts in celebration when one person owns his or her sin, sees the need of a savior, and cries out for grace.**

Jesus had begun this round of teaching with stories about animals and coins. Now he is going to talk about people. More specifically, rebellious individuals like you and like me. The parable of the prodigal son is probably the most famous parable. It may be very familiar to you, but consider two things: (1) Don't forget that Jesus is still sitting with broken sinners, the religious gathered around him; (2) A parable is told with the intention of sweeping up listeners (and readers) into the story and finding touch points within that strongly resonate. So don't read the prodigal son story like any other story. Look to see how it speaks to *your* story.

And [Jesus] said, "There was a man who had two sons. And the younger of them said to his father, 'Father, give me the share of property that is coming to me.' And he divided his property between them. Not many days later, the younger son gathered all he had and took a journey into a far country, and there he squandered his property in reckless living. And when he had spent everything, a severe famine arose in that country, and he began to be in need. So he went and hired himself out to one of the citizens of that country, who sent him into his fields to feed pigs. And he was longing to be fed with the pods that the pigs ate, and no one gave him anything.

"But when he came to himself, he said, 'How many of my father's hired servants have more than enough bread, but I perish here with hunger! I will arise and go to my father, and I will say to him, 'Father, I have sinned against heaven and before you. I am no longer worthy to be called your son. Treat me as one of your hired servants.' And he arose and came to his father. But while he was still a long way off, his father saw him and felt compassion, and ran and embraced him and kissed him. And the son said to him, 'Father, I have sinned against heaven and before you. I am no longer worthy to be called your son.' But the father said to his servants, 'Bring quickly the best robe, and put it on him, and put a ring on his hand, and shoes on his feet. And bring the fattened calf and kill it, and let us eat and celebrate. For this my son was dead, and is alive again; he was lost, and is found.' And they began to celebrate.

"Now his older son was in the field, and as he came and drew near to the house, he heard music and dancing. And he called one of the servants and asked what these things meant. And he said to him, 'Your brother has come, and your father has killed the fattened calf, because he has received him back safe and sound.' But he was angry and refused to go in. His father came out and entreated him, but he answered his father, 'Look, these many years I have served you, and I never disobeyed your command, yet you never gave me a young goat, that I might celebrate with my friends. But when this son of yours came, who has devoured your property with prostitutes, you killed the fattened calf for him!' And he said to him, 'Son, you are always with me, and all that is mine is yours. It was fitting to celebrate and be glad, for this your brother was dead, and is alive; he was lost, and is found.'"

Luke 15:11–32

If there is a Bible that everyone, regardless of age, should own, I believe it is *The Jesus Storybook Bible*.[2] It is wonderful. I read it regularly to my kids, and even by myself. I particularly love how it wraps up the parable of the prodi-gal son: "Jesus told people this story to show them what God is like. And to show people what they are like. So they could know, however far they ran, however well they hid, however lost they were—it wouldn't matter. Because God's children could never run too far, or be too lost, for God to find them."

Can this really be how God is with his most rebellious, ungrateful, and utterly sinful children? Remember, the son requested his inheritance *before* his father died. In effect, he was saying, "I don't care about you. I don't even care about us. All I want is your cash. You're dead to me."

The father, who might have counted the boy's fingers and toes when he was a baby, sang to him night after night, nursed him when he was sick, perhaps taught him how to write his name, watched his son walk out the front door, with a pocket full of money and a mind full of dreams and a life "free" from his dad, rules, and his family.

The son's heart grew hard as stone. It was almost like he didn't feel anything. The words of Mister Rogers seem appropriate here:

> Part of the problem with the word "disabilities" is that it immediately suggests an inability to see or hear or walk or do many other things that many of us take for granted. But what of people who can't feel? Or talk about their feelings? Or manage their feelings in constructive ways? What of people who aren't able to form close and strong relationships? And what of people who cannot find fulfillment in their lives, or those who have lost hope, who live in disappointment and bitterness and find in life no joy, no love? These, it seems to me, are the real disabilities.[3]

The younger son exchanged the inheritance property for cash and lived what Jesus called a "reckless," or literally "senseless," life. It doesn't take much for any of us to imagine what recklessness looks like. One thing we do know is that based on verse 30, the son hired prostitutes. Women, partying, wild nights. Indulging in the lust of the flesh, the lust of the eyes, and the pride of life. It seems that the son, seeking love, affection, and acceptance, would rather pay for those comforts in a consumer relationship than enjoy what was already given to him by his father.

But soon the money ran out, famine struck the land, and the only job for this Jewish runaway was feeding pigs. This would've sounded completely repulsive and yet like sweet victory to the Pharisees and scribes listening to Jesus. *The pigs are getting fatter, and he's getting skinnier by the day,* they must have thought. *Serves him right. After all, you reap what you sow. He made his bed, now he has to lie in it.*

But after coming to his senses, the son plans his I'm-sorry speech and heads home. What will his father say? Will he be run off the property? Will he truly get what he deserves? We can only imagine that he's dirty, disheveled, and malnourished. He might have been ready to assume the role of a leper and cover his mouth and shout "Unclean!" But then comes the most unexpected verse in the Bible: "But while he was still a long way off, his father saw him and felt compassion, and ran and embraced him and kissed him" (Luke 15:20). The way *The Jesus Storybook Bible* describes this moment happens to be an excellent translation from the original Greek: "His dad runs to him, throws his arms around him, and can't stop kissing him." That's right, "can't stop kissing him." And then the shouting begins. But not the kind we would have expected. There's no "Where have you been?! How could you waste my money? Do you realize what you've done to the family name?" We don't sense any anger or hurt feelings. Instead there are shouts of joy and excitement as the father calls for his best robe and shoes to be given to the son, and a fattened calf for a feast, as though a major holiday were about to be celebrated. A ring, possibly one that bore the family crest, was placed on his finger. Strike up the band! Get everyone here! This is not just another day! This is *the* day! "My boy is home! My heart is thrilled!"

The scribes and Pharisees, the rule keepers, would have been absolutely shocked at this point of the parable. Though more space in Scripture is dedicated to describing the son, this story says a lot more about the father than the rebel. The only thing more reckless than the son's rebellion is the father's grace. This is what grace actually looks like—it's extravagant and completely over the top. It appears wasteful, excessive, and totally senseless.

Jesus ends the parable by shifting the attention to the other brother, who clearly represents the Pharisees and scribes. The older son is enraged over the music, dancing, and outright celebrating over the brother who has come home. He goes to the father and refuses to call the restored sibling "brother" but simply "this son of yours." The father corrects the son, and the story ends with the father entreating the older brother to come back in to the party and enjoy grace.

Friends, the God of heaven is a God who delights in forgiving your sins and burying them in the bottom of the sea, never to emerge again. God specializes in separating your sins from you as far as the east is from the west, never to be seen again. In love for you, God *forgets* your sins, forgives, pays your debts, and treats you as if you were as blameless, spotless, and loved as Jesus. He stands, inviting you right now both to his present and future love.

Laughter, Chalz, the Worst Day of My Life, and the Beginning of My Salvation

Let me bring this a bit more up close and share a personal story of God's grace in my life.

If there's anything I enjoy in this world, it is laughing and making others laugh. It has always been this way for me. I remember the morning in fifth grade when I got to school and realized there would be talent-show tryouts that day. Without any preparation, I got up in front of my class and rattled off a famous comedian's monologue I had already memorized. Later, I ended up winning the school-wide talent show.

A few years later, another opportunity came up that seemed like a chance for fun and laughs. It turned out to be the worst day of my life.

> **Another opportunity came up that seemed like a chance for fun and laughs. It turned out to be the worst day of my life.**

I was in the eighth grade, and always seemed to be in trouble for fighting, vandalism, and dabbling in whatever sneak-drinking I could. I was failing all of my classes except typing, which I was barely passing.

A candy-selling fund raiser was taking place at the time, and a girl dared me to steal another student's box of candy.

I knew the stakes were high, but I also knew that laughing with my friends as we stuffed ourselves with chocolate was totally worth it. So I carefully slid the box of candy out from under his desk and slipped what had to be a hundred Reese's Peanut Butter Cups into my bag. Then, at the start of third-period phys ed, I handed out Reese's Cups to all my buddies in the locker room. Everyone had a huge laugh and got a good sugar buzz before playing basketball.

A half hour later, my principal, with whom I had already had a few previous encounters, showed up and asked to speak with me. "Alex, did you steal someone's fund-raiser candy last period?" I looked squarely at her—the law, the standard, the person who had the power to ruin my life—and boldly replied, "No." In no time I was escorted back to my locker and watched as my coach opened my backpack. There they were—fifty or so peanut butter cups left. The look on my principal's face was absolute anger.

We went to her office and I sat down in my regular chair by the window and readied myself to get my typical in-school suspension. I got a deathblow instead. She called my father, William ("Chalz"), who worked in downtown Atlanta at Georgia Power, out of a business meeting, and said, "You need to come for Alex and take him home."

I cannot tell you how scary that moment was. I was dead. I just knew it. I thought of the last few privileges I still had at home and knew they would be gone. No more fun things for me. More than anything, I feared what my dad would say. He came to the principal's office, looked at me, and without a word took me home. He led me to my bedroom, took away my stereo, and told me only that I was grounded.

It was a Wednesday, which meant my mom would be going to church that evening for orchestra practice. After sitting in my room for hours, bored to tears, I asked if I could go to church that night. My puzzled parents agreed, but warned about anything going wrong. Sure enough, at the end of the evening, I got in a fight and broke the kid's glasses before pushing him in some bushes and making a quick escape to my mom's car. When she asked how church had gone for me, I answered simply, "Oh, fine."

Back home, I was already in bed at ten o'clock when the phone rang. My gut sank. Two minutes later, my door flew open. It was my dad. "You got in a fight? You broke someone's glasses?"

"Yes, but he started it."

My dad didn't buy it. (I am still grounded, in fact.)

Suspended from school the next day, I was surprised when my dad told me we would be doing something around lunchtime and that I should dress nicely. With few, if any, words between us, we drove downtown to a tall, beautiful, black cylindrical tower called the Peachtree Plaza. (Practically everything in Atlanta is named "Peachtree.") At the very top is an excellent restaurant known as the Sun Dial. It revolves so that you can get a panoramic view of the city while you eat a wonderful meal. We got in the super-fun elevator and went straight to the top floor. After being seated, my dad ordered two filets and we sat in silence and looked over Atlanta—"The city too busy to hate," its slogan since the 1960s. It was a perfectly clear day, and I remember feeling scared and confused at the same time. *What in the world is going to happen? This is crazy. I'm the worst kid in school. I'm failing my classes. I lie about everything. I'm so angry. I certainly don't know who I am. All I want is to be liked by a crowd of people who I think are cool. How am I even sitting right here? I should be doing community service.*

Toward the end of our steak lunch, my dad finally broke the deafening silence. "Alex, I love you. How you're living is breaking our hearts. Our family is in a constant uproar over decisions you're making. I simply want the best for you. Think about your life. Come to your senses. Now, what do you want for dessert?"

That's it. No threats. No long lecture. To the best of my memory, that was all he said about the incident.

I didn't become a believer that day, but I honestly believed in that moment—more clearly than ever before—that my dad loved me, that he wanted to be with me. My dad wanted me.

If salvation is a process of coming to the light, that day I took my first step, because kindness really does lead to repentance. And, you know, I laugh a lot more often and a lot louder than ever before.

—— 4 ——

Jesus Loves **Me** (Part 2)
This I Know,
for the Bible Tells Me So

"There's a crack in everything. That's how the
light gets in."[1]

—Leonard Cohen

I'm a pastor. And almost every Sunday throughout the year,
I preach the gospel. I've developed certain personal routines
and rituals that I do throughout the year. For me, early Sunday mornings involve coffee, yogurt, tons of prayer, reading
my notes, the Book of Common Prayer, and music. For the
last year, every Sunday morning before church I turn on a
playlist that I call "Sunday Mornin' Comin' Down." The first
track I listen to every week without fail is "Sunday Mornin'
Comin' Down" by Johnny Cash. I love Johnny Cash. For

years I even had a dog named Cash. (RIP, buddy.) The way Johnny put things is just phenomenal, especially this song that talks of a rough Saturday night for a lonely, tired soul who drinks a couple of beers for breakfast and wants to get stoned to dull the pain, the weight, the heaviness, of Sunday morning coming down.

I'm drawn to this song because it's honestly what so many people in my city wake up feeling like, and I've got good news to tell them.

Why is Sunday so hard for so many people? Why is Cash's experience one that resonates with countless people? Because Sunday is the day that represents hope, life, and love for this world, and yet it doesn't feel like that all over our country, especially in many churches. Folks show up hoping to hear about grace and redemption, but often find a club that has closed its membership and is content to use insider language. What is the hope for the world, not just on Sunday, but every moment between now and the moment we take our first steps through the gates of heaven? The personal love of God felt in the soul of one of his image-bearers.

God did not simply remain in heaven and write his plans and will in the sky and coolly observe us from a distance. His love required that he become incarnate in Jesus. The parables that we just looked at are stunning pictures of incredible grace. But Jesus did more than paint beautiful images of the personal and passionate nature of the gospel. He *intentionally* submerged his hands completely in the sewers of our world to touch, heal, redeem, and restore it back to the way it should be. John says, "Let us not love in word or talk but in deed and in truth" (1 John 3:18). That is precisely what Jesus did. He *did* something right there, on the spot, for individuals right in front of him.

There are a few ways people encounter Jesus in the Gospels. Some come and fall at his feet, some go find him in the middle of the night, some are brought by friends, some happen to be on the side of the road as he passes by (or up in a tree!), and sometimes he just goes looking for someone.

Our First Major Loss: Adam

In 2007, my wife and I moved to London so that I could pursue a master of arts degree in biblical interpretation from the London School of Theology. We lived there on campus in the cozy northwestern neighborhood of Northwood. It was an exciting time for us, especially because we were pregnant with our first child. We wondered what it would be like to have our first baby born in London, of all places.

One night, Jana woke up and knew something wasn't right. She had a sick feeling that she was losing the baby. We were scared and called the doctor. I fought back tears all night, just hoping and praying that everything would be okay. The next morning, a Sunday, we walked up the street to the Tube station and rode a few stops down to the local hospital. It was about eight when we arrived, but the place looked completely abandoned. We walked down several dark halls, until finally finding a woman at a desk who told us we were at the wrong place. It was like we were living a nightmare.

From there we took a cab to the correct hospital. We waited for several hours before we could see the doctor. Let me tell you, praying without ceasing in those hours felt as natural as breathing. When Jana finally got hooked up to a sonogram machine, we searched for our baby and saw him! Our relief was shattered, though, when the doctor said with a stone-cold face, "There's no heartbeat. It's gone." I looked up at Jana and saw what I still believe to be the most heartrending expression I have ever witnessed. I saw her soul in her face, and it was tearing from east to west. Sadness, devastation, brokenness set in on the two of us. The only thing we could do was make an appointment for a D&C and go home.

Outside Watford Hospital it was raining now. There we were, alone in a big city in a foreign country, with no umbrella or money for a cab ride back to our flat, trying to process news that had shaken us to our core. We walked in silence, only sniffling as our tears and the rain ran together. But just before reaching the underground Tube station, I sensed God speaking to me. (I use those words very seriously, for I know how serious it is to say, "God told me.")

Alex, you will reap what you sow. Your heart is tilled up. You can either sow seeds of hatred, distrust, and resentment, or you can sow the seeds of faith, hope, and love. Your future is being shaped in this moment.

I stopped and told Jana what I thought God was saying to me.

"What should we do?" I asked.

"Let's sow right seeds," she replied.

A few days later the procedure was finished, and I spoke with my dad on the phone about the whole experience.

"What was your baby's name?" he asked.

"Honestly, Dad, I don't know. We hadn't decided before this happened."

"I think you should name him Adam."

"What?" I replied.

"It's important to know his name," he said. "He was your son."

Adam wasn't an "it." He was our son. Of course Jana and I grieved in the days and months after going through what so many others have also endured. We asked questions, and had major bouts with doubt. But every June 1, we think of little Adam. I have his middle name picked out and look forward to telling him his middle name one day in heaven.

When Jana and I returned to the United States, we purchased a home and I planted my first church. One morning, while Jana was at work and I was writing a sermon at our dining room table, I slumped into really missing little Adam. I flipped my Bible open to the last pages of Job to again see how God spoke to a man in incredible pain and suffering. What I found there was a God with no answers for Job, just questions. "Brace yourself like a man," God told Job. "I will question you, and you shall answer me. 'Where were you when I laid the earth's foundation?'" (Job 38:3–4 NIV).

In that moment, I was so angry with God that I threw my Bible at the wall. "*That* is how you comfort someone, God? You are a bully!" And then I put my head on the table and wept.

God oftentimes does not give me answers to my questions. Rather, he gives me himself.

After several minutes, though, the questions God asked Job began to wash over me and give me the perspective I needed. I realized God's questions to Job (and to me) were not intended to say, "Shut up. Don't you know how powerful I am?" No. The questions were intended to point me beyond myself and my own experience into the realm of the divine. Before long, I began to realize that God oftentimes does not give me answers to my questions. Rather, he gives me himself. I then began to meditate on the cross of Jesus and see more than I'd ever seen before. I knew God not only had suffered for me, but he was currently, presently, suffering *with* me. In that moment Jesus, through the presence of the Holy Spirit, was weeping *with* me.

But was this feeling I had real? Does God really feel that way when we hurt? What sort of evidence is there in the Bible for this?

Mark 2: Through the Roof for Jesus

Once you've met Jesus, there's usually an indescribable desire to have others encounter him. In the New Testament, we are told about four men who bring their paralyzed friend to Jesus. We don't know if they were already followers of Jesus, but they were obviously impressed with his power and apparently presumed his grace would collide with their faith and help their friend.

> And when [Jesus] returned to Capernaum after some days, it was reported that he was at home. And many were gathered together, so that there was no more room, not even at the door. And he was preaching the word to them. And they came, bringing to him a paralytic carried by four men. And when they could not get near him because of the crowd, they removed the roof above him, and when they had made an opening, they let down the bed on which the paralytic lay. And when Jesus saw their faith, he said to the paralytic,

"Son, your sins are forgiven." Now some of the scribes were sitting there, questioning in their hearts, "Why does this man speak like that? He is blaspheming! Who can forgive sins but God alone?" And immediately Jesus, perceiving in his spirit that they thus questioned within themselves, said to them, "Why do you question these things in your hearts? Which is easier, to say to the paralytic, 'Your sins are forgiven,' or to say, 'Rise, take up your bed and walk'? But that you may know that the Son of Man has authority on earth to forgive sins"—he said to the paralytic—"I say to you, rise, pick up your bed, and go home." And he rose and immediately picked up his bed and went out before them all, so that they were all amazed and glorified God, saying, "We never saw anything like this!"

Mark 2:1–12

As Scripture tells us, Jesus had packed out a small house and was teaching the locals from Capernaum, the fishing village where he spent the majority of his time. Scholars estimate that there were between six hundred and twelve hundred residents at the time. Excavations show homes in which they could fit fifty persons at most if they stood close together (the longest span in excavated homes is eighteen feet). Truly a small town with small houses.

Mark's gospel repeatedly alludes to Jesus' popularity by mentioning crowds (more than thirty times in nearly seven hundred verses). People were constantly coming to him for teaching, healing, and miracles. In this passage from chapter 2, Jesus was inside the house "preaching the word to them," and the crowd was so big it actually spilled out the front door.

Homes usually had some sort of stairs outside that led to the roof. And the roof of single-story homes back then was sturdy enough to walk on. They were normally made of branches and brushes spread over the roof's wooden beams and covered with dried mud. Oftentimes, people would relax on their roof in order to get out of the muggy house. They could get fresh air, dry their laundry, eat meals, and wind down.

In this account, the four men bring their friend onto the roof and start digging through the mud and branches in a section of it. I'm sure as dust and dirt began to sift into the room, and beams of sunlight pierced through, the crowd became restless. When everyone looked up, they would have seen four hopeful (maybe grinning) faces looking down. Quite an interruption to say the least! But they weren't finished yet. They lowered their paralyzed friend on the mat in front of Jesus. Can you imagine the looks the paralytic and Jesus exchanged?

The friends were demonstrating a dangerous, controversial, even reckless faith in Jesus. Seeing that kind of faith, Jesus forgave the man's sins.[2] The scribes grumbled about this apparently blasphemous statement. Only God can forgive sins, they said. But Jesus demonstrated his authority by merely giving the word, and the paralytic received his strength back and immediately began to walk.

Christian, please understand this: When Jesus says you are forgiven, *you are forgiven.* When Jesus says you are loved, *you are loved.* When Jesus says you are free, *you are free.*

Fishing at a Well—John 4

The next Bible story I want to highlight is when Jesus, the fisher of men, went fishing at a well. It starts with Jesus sitting down in the middle of the day next to the famous well where Jacob had watered his flocks years before. Jesus knew that morning whom he would encounter and what would happen. Picture it. It's a hot, dusty, arid land, and Jesus is all alone by the well. He bows his head, wipes the sweat off his brow, and then looks up and sees the silhouette of a woman in the distance. It's her. He knows her. She won't know him or recognize him, but he has had her rescue planned from before the foundation of the world. She arrives at the well, and the story picks up here:

> A woman from Samaria came to draw water. Jesus said to her, "Give me a drink." (For his disciples had gone away into the city to buy food.) The Samaritan woman said to him, "How is it that you, a Jew, ask for a drink from me, a woman of Samaria?" (For Jews have no dealings with Samaritans.) Jesus answered her, "If you knew the gift of God, and who it is that is saying to you, 'Give me a drink,' you would have asked him, and he would have given you living water." The woman said to him, "Sir, you have nothing to draw water with, and the well is deep. Where do you get that living water? Are you greater than our father Jacob? He gave us the well and drank from it himself, as did his sons and his livestock." Jesus said to her, "Everyone who drinks of this water will be thirsty again, but whoever drinks of the water that I will give him will never be thirsty again. The water that I will give him will become in him a spring of water welling up to eternal life." The woman said to him, "Sir, give me this water, so that I will not be thirsty or have to come here to draw water."
>
> Jesus said to her, "Go, call your husband, and come here." The woman answered him, "I have no husband." Jesus said

to her, "You are right in saying, 'I have no husband'; for you have had five husbands, and the one you now have is not your husband. What you have said is true." The woman said to him, "Sir, I perceive that you are a prophet. Our fathers worshiped on this mountain, but you say that in Jerusalem is the place where people ought to worship." Jesus said to her, "Woman, believe me, the hour is coming when neither on this mountain nor in Jerusalem will you worship the Father. You worship what you do not know; we worship what we know, for salvation is from the Jews. But the hour is coming, and is now here, when the true worshipers will worship the Father in spirit and truth, for the Father is seeking such people to worship him. God is spirit, and those who worship him must worship in spirit and truth." The woman said to him, "I know that Messiah is coming (he who is called Christ). When he comes, he will tell us all things." Jesus said to her, "I who speak to you am he."

Just then his disciples came back. They marveled that he was talking with a woman, but no one said, "What do you seek?" or, "Why are you talking with her?" So the woman left her water jar and went away into town and said to the people, "Come, see a man who told me all that I ever did. Can this be the Christ?" They went out of the town and were coming to him.

John 4:7–30

Of all the theological intricacies that John chapter 4 presents, this stands out for our purposes: Jesus is found *speaking* with this woman. Here he is again, breaking the rules and pushing the boundaries in order to love somebody. Back then it was a social taboo to even be in the company of a woman like this. The Samaritans were despised because their ancestors were Jews who had intermingled with other religious parties and embraced their various forms of idolatry. Recall that on one occasion, the disciples asked Jesus if they were to call down fire on the Samaritans (Luke 9:54).

Look at the interest Jesus shows in this woman's wellbeing. He sits with her at the well and answers her questions about God and worship, and demonstrates that neither place nor race defines one's identity before God. Beyond the theology of this, savor the fact that he's taking her seriously and giving her straight answers. He provokes her interest by asking her to give him some water, but then says, "You actually need the water I have." Essentially he's saying, "I'm thirsty, but my dry throat cannot compare to your parched soul." And now that he has her attention, Jesus shows he is not out to win a theology debate. He wants to win *her.* How do I know? Because he goes straight to her heart and tells her, "Go and get your husband," knowing this would send her backpedaling. She says she has no husband, and then Jesus acknowledges that she's had several husbands and the man she is with now is not her husband.

Jesus is found speaking with this woman. Here he is again, breaking the rules and pushing the boundaries in order to love somebody.

For Jesus, answering her questions about traditions for worship shows his kindness. Confronting her sin, brokenness, and shame—no matter how personal—shows his *love.*

I've heard sin defined in this way: Sin is an exaggeration or diminishment of what God calls "good." How the Samaritan woman ended up with so many partners, we don't know. What we do see is the diminishment of the gift of sex and relationship. Jesus wants what is best for her, which includes being loved—the kind of love that produces the fruits of faith, repentance, and life with God.

The woman perceives he is a prophet and begins to drink the water of everlasting life for the first time. John doesn't record anything about Jesus belaboring the point of her sin. Nor does he record her wallowing in unbearable shame. What we see is that she knows that *he* knows what hurts within her, and he is there to pour infinite amounts of living water on her parched soul. Can you see the gentleness Jesus shows toward someone in the middle of her sin? He gives her dignity. He gives her respect. He gives her grace upon grace.

Right now, he has the same living water for you and your thirsty soul. Drink the water. Receive the grace. Believe he loves you this very minute.

Shouting Into a Cave—John 11

We could look at countless examples of God's unspeakable love throughout John's gospel, but this one—the story of Lazarus rising from the dead—more than suffices.

> Now a certain man was ill, Lazarus of Bethany, the village of Mary and her sister Martha. It was Mary who anointed the Lord with ointment and wiped his feet with her hair, whose brother Lazarus was ill. So the sisters sent to him, saying, "Lord, he whom you love is ill." But when Jesus heard it he said, "This illness does not lead to death. It is for the glory of God, so that the Son of God may be glorified through it."

Now Jesus loved Martha and her sister and Lazarus. So, when he heard that Lazarus was ill, he stayed two days longer in the place where he was. Then after this he said to the disciples, "Let us go to Judea again." The disciples said to him, "Rabbi, the Jews were just now seeking to stone you, and are you going there again?" Jesus answered, "Are there not twelve hours in the day? If anyone walks in the day, he does not stumble, because he sees the light of this world. But if anyone walks in the night, he stumbles, because the light is not in him." After saying these things, he said to them, "Our friend Lazarus has fallen asleep, but I go to awaken him." The disciples said to him, "Lord, if he has fallen asleep, he will recover." Now Jesus had spoken of his death, but they thought that he meant taking rest in sleep. Then Jesus told them plainly, "Lazarus has died, and for your sake I am glad that I was not there, so that you may believe. But let us go to him." So Thomas, called the Twin, said to his fellow disciples, "Let us also go, that we may die with him."

Now when Jesus came, he found that Lazarus had already been in the tomb four days. Bethany was near Jerusalem, about two miles off, and many of the Jews had come to Martha and Mary to console them concerning their brother. So when Martha heard that Jesus was coming, she went and met him, but Mary remained seated in the house. Martha said to Jesus, "Lord, if you had been here, my brother would not have died. But even now I know that whatever you ask from God, God will give you." Jesus said to her, "Your brother will rise again." Martha said to him, "I know that he will rise again in the resurrection on the last day." Jesus said to her, "I am the resurrection and the life. Whoever believes in me, though he die, yet shall he live, and everyone who lives and believes in me shall never die. Do you believe this?" She said to him, "Yes, Lord; I believe that you are the Christ, the Son of God, who is coming into the world."

When she had said this, she went and called her sister Mary, saying in private, "The Teacher is here and is calling for you." And when she heard it, she rose quickly and went to him. Now Jesus had not yet come into the village, but was still in the place where Martha had met him. When the Jews who were with her in the house, consoling her, saw Mary rise quickly and go out, they followed her, supposing that she was going to the tomb to weep there. Now when Mary came to where Jesus was and saw him, she fell at his feet, saying to him, "Lord, if you had been here, my brother would not have died." When Jesus saw her weeping, and the Jews who had come with her also weeping, he was deeply moved in his spirit and greatly troubled. And he said, "Where have you laid him?" They said to him, "Lord, come and see." Jesus wept. So the Jews said, "See how he loved him!" But some of them said, "Could not he who opened the eyes of the blind man also have kept this man from dying?"

Then Jesus, deeply moved again, came to the tomb. It was a cave, and a stone lay against it. Jesus said, "Take away the stone." Martha, the sister of the dead man, said to him, "Lord, by this time there will be an odor, for he has been dead four days." Jesus said to her, "Did I not tell you that if you believed you would see the glory of God?" So they took away the stone. And Jesus lifted up his eyes and said, "Father, I thank you that you have heard me. I knew that you always hear me, but I said this on account of the people standing around, that they may believe that you sent me." When he had said these things, he cried out with a loud voice, "Lazarus, come out." The man who had died came out, his hands and feet bound with linen strips, and his face wrapped with a cloth. Jesus said to them, "Unbind him, and let him go."

John 11:1–44

Notice in the beginning that Jesus is told, "Lord, the one you love is ill." Not "Lord, the one who is trying so hard to be faithful to you and love you and obey you is ill." Here, Jesus was known for one thing: loving his friend, Lazarus. The sisters didn't appeal to any favors that Jesus might owe his friend. Jesus is in debt to no man. Only the mention of his love is recorded.

Curiously, Jesus intentionally waits two days to travel the fairly short distance to Bethany, only to find a brokenhearted family who had buried Lazarus in a nearby cave four days earlier. When Jesus speaks with the sisters, John records some of the rawest, most vulnerable emotion the New Testament has to offer. Certainly, it is here we see how human and how divine Jesus is. Indeed, theologians point to this Scripture passage when they talk about the incarnation—Jesus being truly God and truly man, the God-man. He possesses the incomprehensible power to raise the dead, and yet, reading carefully, you can sense deep emotions running through his body and soul. John writes, "When Jesus saw her weeping . . . he was deeply moved in his spirit and greatly troubled" (11:33). F. F. Bruce, the famous British New Testament scholar, notes that John used the verb *embrimaomi*, "translated here 'became deeply agitated,' [which] means literally 'snort (with indignation).'" Bruce adds, "So powerful was Jesus' emotional reaction to the spectacle that he 'shook' (literally, 'troubled himself') under the force of it."[3] The God-man from Galilee not only experiences anger at sin and its consequences ("the wages of sin is death," Romans

6:23) but also deep sadness. Jesus experienced what each of us is bound to face: losing someone we love.

The pain, the agony, the undoing of what God designed in the garden *shook* Jesus. He cried so intensely that even those standing by commented, "Look how he loved him." When words run out, tears speak, for they are oftentimes the language of the soul.

But death would not get the last word. Requesting the stone be rolled back, and with the unnecessary comment about the stench of a decaying body, Jesus lifts up a loud voice and shouts into the cave, "Lazarus, come out!" Jesus' voice undoubtedly echoed. Deep calling to deep, indeed. And when the disciples loosened Lazarus' grave clothing, what a sight it must have been for Lazarus to look out of the cave and see a tearstained face, his friend full of love and limitless power, grinning at him, welcoming him back to life. Oh, the love and power of Jesus.

Jesus' voice spoke creation into being. That same voice rang out to Lazarus and is now calling to you, "Come to me, my beloved."

Jesus shook hands with death and death's hand withered.

Jesus looked sin in the eye and sin went blind.

Jesus went toe to toe with religion and broke religion's back.

Jesus whispered one word in the ears of Satan and Satan went deaf.

Jesus spoke and the demons' tongues were tied.

Jesus' presence paralyzed rebellion.

Jesus' resurrection put shame to shame.

With Jesus' love for us, we don't have to dread Sunday mornin' comin' down. It can and should feel different.

5

Jesus Loves Me (Part 3) This I Know, for the Bible Tells Me So

"If you do not know that Jesus loves you, you lack the brightest star that can cheer the night of sickness."[1]

—Charles Spurgeon

"If the essence of Christianity is neither a creed, nor a code, nor a cult, what is it? It is Christ! It is not primarily a system of any kind; it is a person, and a personal relationship to that Person."[2]

—John Stott

It is wonderful to know who Jesus is, the nature of God's incredible love for the world, and the beautiful parables and stories of Jesus interacting with people in Scripture. But what does the Bible say about Jesus' love for you and for me? To answer this question, we have to go back to the very beginning.

In Genesis, humankind is made in the image of God, and our parents, Adam and Eve, serve as our representatives. When God made us, he was pleased with us. But then sin broke into the world and fractured everything. Humans became violent, fearful, shameful, sinful, distorted, and marred down to the very fabric of our DNA. We became offensive before God's perfect justice. Yet we are created in his image.

Does the word *offensive* strike you as harsh? As Anselm, a profound theologian of the eleventh century, said in a rhetorical conversation with Boso, "You have not considered how great your sin is." Sin is rebellion, an offense against God.

But as you've seen, the story does not end there. Reckless love invades. Not only does Jesus love the world, the church, and humanity in general, but he loves *you*—individually, personally. He loves *individual* stories, each with his or her unique skin color, fingerprint, and voice.

To personally receive, own, and extend this love of God for oneself and others requires a journey involving sober, honest prayer; close attention to the Bible; and believing the impossible. This is not a beckoning into blind naïveté. Neither is this a plunge into existential emotionalism or a plea to drive down a road that dead-ends into an eternal cul-de-sac of boring religious duties. Instead, understanding this single truth will change you forever, leaving you more speechless, breathless, and in time, more selfless than you ever thought possible. Theologian Paul Tillich says that "encountering God means encountering transcendent security and transcendent eternity. He who participates in God participates in eternity. But in order to participate in him you must be accepted by him and you must have accepted his acceptance of you."[3]

I'd like to first show you how far God is willing to go.

You see, even today the love of Jesus confounds society's extremes—the clean and the unclean, the insiders and outsiders, the sterile and the fertile, the religious and the irreligious. The upstanding man who thinks he doesn't need Jesus' love is frustrated by the gospel message because his flawless religious performances and nitpicking morals are deemed crass by the writers of Scripture. They are "garbage" (Philippians 3:8 NIV) and "filthy rags" (Isaiah 64:6 NIV). The self-righteous, self-sufficient moralist who thinks he is heavy enough to tip the scales of judgment actually weighs less than a feather. That's right. On his best day, he still comes up short.

> **Even today the love of Jesus confounds society's extremes—the clean and the unclean, the insiders and outsiders, the sterile and the fertile, the religious and the irreligious.**

On the other extreme is the man who experiments with drug after drug, sleeps with woman after woman, spends time in jail cell after jail cell, whose mind, heart, and soul resemble a septic tank. To this person, the love of Jesus appears scandalous, outrageous, too good to be true, even reckless. Even so, Jesus says, "[God] is kind to ungrateful and evil men" (Luke 6:35 NASB).

Eighteen Months

Now I want to show you whom Jesus loved *first,* at least as far as his earthly ministry and chronological time is concerned. During his last night with the disciples, he said "I have loved you just as the Father has loved me" (John 15:9 NJB). Did you catch that simile? It's a big deal. Read that line again slowly and put all the weight on "just as." With God's perfect love, Jesus *loved* his disciples.

By the time Jesus actually identified and called the Twelve from the larger group of his followers, half of his earthly ministry was over. This means that these few men had little more than eighteen months of training for the monumental task to which they were called. There was no second string, no backup players, no plan B if the Twelve should fail. These men were called to be converted disciples and to serve until the searing end. Eventually, all but one gave their lives in martyrdom because Jesus' love was more valuable than the breath in their lungs, their retirement plans, or their personal ambitions. The love of Christ controlled them (2 Corinthians 5:14).

Four Groups

The gospel writers arranged the lists of disciples in groups. Group 1 always has Peter at the head of the list, followed by Andrew, James, and John. Group 2 has Philip first, followed by Bartholomew, Matthew, and Thomas. Group 3 is more distant, and its members are rarely mentioned. The only member of this group we know much about is Judas Iscariot—because of his betrayal of Jesus. Though there were twelve apostles, only three seem to have been intimately related to Jesus. The others seemed to have somewhat lesser degrees of personal familiarity with him.

Although Jesus was considered a rabbi, or great teacher, he did not follow all of the traditional customs of the day to a T. Rather, in significant ways he blazed his own new path toward making disciples. Here are a few examples of this rabbi who transcended the customary boxes of the day:

- Rabbis usually had one disciple. Jesus had twelve.
- Typically students would go through a lengthy application process that most could not pass.[4] Jesus *sought out* his disciples instead of waiting for applications.
- Rabbis leaned on others' authority for teaching. Jesus spoke on *his own authority* and strongly impressed the learned religious community.[5]
- Those that pursued discipleship often came from the upper echelon of the religious society. Jesus' disciples differed. In fact, what is remarkable is that—contrary to what television documentaries and stained-glass windows portray—these twelve are not known for their superior backgrounds, miracles performed, or great faith and unwavering trust in God.

Jesus Picked the No-Names

The disciples are not memorable for their sharp-mindedness, their humility before God, or their deep love for other people. They were not in the right place at the right time, with all the dazzling credentials that successful religious people tend to adore and reward. They would not have been admired for their ability to hold their tongues, or for possessing leadership qualities that matched today's Fortune 500 CEOs. They were not altar boys, seminary professors, or worship pastors. Prior to meeting Jesus, these men were not studying theology or leadership materials. No, this very human motley crew was comprised of pretentious, self-centered, and self-deprecating scalawags, and included a murderer, extortionists, and racists who later doubted events they had witnessed with their own eyes. They were thieves who went on to prove themselves to be prone to cowardice and violence, small-mindedness, faithlessness, and even proclivity to be mama's boys from time to time. If this view upsets some, I'm not looking for a fight. I just want to show who the *real* hero of the story is. After all, does a king share his throne?

We need to let go of any fanciful walk-on-water, demigod ideas about the disciples. These were men with clay feet like you and me. They were slow to discard their old natures. In Mark's gospel, they valued popularity (1:36–37), power and position (10:35–41), unhealthy competition (9:33–34), and had wrong ideas about wealth (10:24–26).

Jesus, as their rabbi, had a God-sized objective for their lives. He wasn't interested in employing a twelve-man traveling fishing crew. Jesus was out to make disciples—men with depth in their minds, love in their hearts, and strong spines, all in the name of truth. Men who merely would put their money where their mouths were, so to speak, and would not ask God to answer someone's prayer, but sought to *be that person's answer to prayer*. Jesus provided plenty of instruction to the disciples, yet when their sinful natures came out in situations, he continued to love them.

If Jesus loved these flawed men, you can trust that he can and does love you.

One fascinating man whom Jesus loved and with whom he spent the bulk of his earthly ministry exemplifies how God's strength is made perfect in weakness (2 Corinthians 12:9). As you read on, you might find yourself identifying with this man who was captivated, transformed, and sustained by the love of Jesus. A man, who, in Christ's strength, mightily altered the face of the world and eternity for countless people: Simon Peter.

Seven Simons

Simon Peter's full name at birth was Simon Bar-Jonah (Matthew 16:17), meaning "Simon son of Jonah or son of John." Details about Peter's parents are lost to history, but they picked a popular name for their son. In the Gospels alone, seven Simons are mentioned. Among the twelve disciples, two were named Simon (Simon Peter and Simon the Zealot). When we see the list of Jesus' siblings, one was named Simon (Matthew 13:55). Judas Iscariot's father was named Simon (John 6:71). Jesus had a meal at the home of a man in Bethany named Simon, who was a leper (Matthew 26:6). A Pharisee named Simon hosted Jesus at a similar meal (Luke 7:36–40). And lastly, the man conscripted to carry Jesus' cross on his way to Calvary was Simon the Cyrene (Mark 15:21).

> **If Jesus loved these flawed men, you can trust that he can and does love you.**

Location: Capernaum

Simon Peter and his brother Andrew were from the town of Bethsaida, but later moved to the city of Capernaum. According to Matthew, we know Jesus set up shop in this propitious city and operated out of it as his primary residence and headquarters for ministry after leaving Nazareth. As mentioned earlier, Capernaum was home to 600 to 1,200 people. It had a fairly well-off commercial district surrounded by fertile lands and plentiful fishing. Flavius Josephus, major first-century Jewish historian, noted that there were at least 230 fishing boats in this small lake called Galilee on any given day.[6] The residents were Jews who labored as fishermen, farmers, artisans, merchants, and officials, including tax collectors.

Occupation: Fisherman

Fishing was an early morning to late night job, and back then it was for a man's man. It was hard work, but could potentially pay well. When Jesus first called Peter, he was working for his dad, Zebedee, who was apparently wealthy enough to hire out day laborers.[7] These men used something resembling a modern cast net. The nets were about twenty feet in diameter and had heavy metal bars attached to the perimeter. This type of fishing was most commonly done in pairs. Peter may have been paired up with his brother Andrew. By wading out just a bit into the lake, the fisherman would have thrown the net in a circular motion, having the net land flat upon the water, and then from that point, let it sink to the bottom. One of the men would swim to the bottom, gather the metal bars together, come back up with the catch, and drag it to the shore.[8] Fishermen typically had broad shoulders, calloused hands, and skin darkened by the sun.

A Polished Nickname

Such an occupation would have toughened Peter. And Jesus, knowing he would be spending a lot of time with him, gave him a nickname in the way that is still common with men today. According to one writer, "Group nicknames thrive within small, insular tribes, gangs, and teams of men who experience regular face-to-face contact, and especially among those male groups that share in a common purpose and set of risks, and together must tackle difficult challenges. Think of military units, criminal organizations like the Mafia, motorcycle gangs, football teams, pioneering and adventure expeditions, and men whose employment isolates them from the outside world (miners, loggers, etc.)."[9]

The first encounter between Jesus and Simon was unusual and packed with significance. John records that Jesus "gazed" at Peter and then gave him a new name, *Cephas* (Say-fuhhs), or *Peter,* meaning "Rock" or "Rocky" (John 1:42). This nickname *Rocky* was extremely intentional, and Jesus' names for Peter serve as signals to us reading the gospel accounts. You could even say that Jesus had a theology of nicknames.

Sometimes Jesus called him Simon and other times he called him Peter. When Jesus used the name *Simon,* it sometimes meant the disciple needed correcting because he wasn't acting like the solid, steadfast, unshakable "Rock" that Jesus called him out to be. That was the case when Jesus prayed in the garden of Gethsemane and asked the disciples to stay awake. "Jesus came and found them sleeping and said to Peter, 'Simon, are you asleep? Could you not watch one hour?'" (Mark 14:37). Perhaps later, when Peter heard his old name, Simon, he cringed, remembering his hypocrisy. Maybe you know how that goes—someone brings up an old name of yours, and it reminds you of poor decisions you made.

Peter's name surfaces more in the Gospels than any other name except *Jesus*. No one speaks as often or is spoken to more than Peter. Of the twelve, no disciple is rebuked by Jesus more often than Peter. And one disciple even rebuked Jesus. Guess who? Yes, Peter (Matthew 16:22). Peter also boldly confessed Christ as the Messiah (Matthew 16:16), while the other eleven remained silent. No other apostle preached with more boldness, passion, and conviction or denied and contested Christ more vehemently.

The Questioner

Simon's nature was to be brash, indecisive, impulsive, and undependable. He tended to make promises he couldn't keep. Peter was also very inquisitive. He asked questions such as how often Jesus expected him to forgive someone, and what reward the disciples would get for the sacrifices they were making to follow him. Peter also frequently wanted the Lord to explain his difficult sayings.

Seeing Your Own Heart

Near the end of John's gospel, he records a couple of conversations that may give you hope regarding the personal nature of Jesus' love. This exchange occurred at the Last Supper:

> Simon Peter said to him, "Lord, where are you going?" Jesus answered him, "Where I am going you cannot follow me now, but you will follow afterward." Peter said to him, "Lord, why can I not follow you now? I will lay down my life for you."
>
> John 13:36–37

Peter can't stand the thought that Jesus' earthly ministry is about to end and that he will soon depart from this world and enter heaven. One can almost see the sweat on Peter's brow, the crumpling of his face, the tears welling up as he swears his unshakable allegiance to Jesus. "Come hell or high water, I will die for you! I don't know about the rest of these guys around the table, but I'm going to the wall for you, Jesus." The thought of being separated from Jesus was too much for Peter.

Certainly, Peter was unprepared for Jesus' reply: "Will you lay down your life for me? Truly, truly, I say to you, the rooster will not crow till you have denied me three times" (John 13:36–38). With these words Jesus exposed the heart-shattering reality that Peter was not as strong as he thought he was. He wouldn't go the distance that night for his rabbi and friend. He couldn't stand up to the opposition. He and Judas would have matching hearts. Both seemed hopeless.

Hopelessness transcends time and characterizes many in our modern world. Walker Percy (1916–1990) addressed this despair in his novels and other writings. In his National Book Award–winning novel *The Moviegoer,* he writes, "Losing hope is not so bad. There's something worse: losing hope and hiding it from yourself."[10]

Peter's experience shows how difficult it is to see deep within ourselves. Just when you think you've progressed beyond the basics of first-level discipleship and are on to more advanced realms of godliness—journeying down the halls of extended prayer, fasting diligently, giving generously, having unshaken integrity and sworn allegiance to God and his will—Jesus asks the soul-exposing, gut-wrenching, heart-stinging question, "Will you really lay down your life for me?" Pause and take a breath.

If Jesus questions our posture of self-sufficiency, it's clear that we were never really prostrate before him in worship to begin with. Peter surely could relate to Jeremiah's words: "Your [own] wickedness . . . has stabbed you to the heart" (Jeremiah 4:18 NJB). That's what wickedness has done to our hearts. But don't worry—we'll come up for air soon. You see, if we don't get a good look at the bad news, we will never understand or appreciate the good news. But first, let's dive deeper.

If we don't get a good look at the bad news, we will never understand or appreciate the good news.

Later that evening, Jesus went with his disciples to the garden of Gethsemane. As mentioned earlier, he asked his inner circle (Peter, James, and John) to be with him while he prayed, but they kept falling asleep. There was Peter, willing to die for his Lord, but he couldn't stay awake for an hour with Jesus. Yes, it had been a long, emotional day, and they had eaten the Passover meal—a knockout combination. But it reminds me of the unfulfilled promises we make before eating the bread and drinking the wine. When Roman soldiers came to arrest Jesus, Peter saw his Lord under threat and rashly drew his sword and cut off the ear of the High Priest's servant. There was Peter again, living up to his word, ready to die for Jesus.

Jesus rebuked Peter's violent hand, healed the wounded servant, and was placed under arrest and led out of the garden. Time passes, and the very real words of Jesus spoken only hours earlier at the supper settle in: "If you were of the world, the world would love you as its own . . . but I chose you . . . therefore the world hates you" (John 15:19). Now Peter must confront his innermost self. He must face the cluster of paradoxes that makes him who he is. Peter tells the truth *and* he lies. He's brave *and* a coward. Peter knows Jesus loves him, but he also knows that the whole world hates him because of Jesus. What will he do? Is Jesus worth all of this? What would you do?

The Look: Some Things Just Can't Be Fixed

Throughout the night, as he watches Jesus from a distance, Peter is questioned three times by three different people (John 18:15, 25–27). Each time he denies any relationship to Jesus. Luke tells us that during the third denial, the dreaded rooster crows and Jesus *looks* at Peter (Luke 22:60–62). This word for "look" (*emblepo*) is more than a glance. As noted above, John uses the same word to describe the first time Jesus looked at Peter (John 1:42). It is a word that means to "gaze knowingly."[11] Jesus gives a prolonged look. He doesn't have a smug "I told you so" look on his face. *Instead, his is the look of love* that says, "I see you for who you are, and I still feel the same about you." And Peter, the Rock, "sinks" for the second time in Jesus' presence—this time in a lake of bitter tears rather than the Sea of Galilee. On this day, Peter has more in common with Judas the betrayer than he (or we) cares to admit. Singer, songwriter, and author Michael Card points out that "the difference between them is that one tries to fix it [through suicide] and the other recognizes that things are beyond fixing."[12]

Early church Father Jerome says, "It could not be that Peter, on whom the light of the world had gazed, should remain in the darkness of denial."[13] Metaphorically reading the words of surgeon Richard Selzer seems appropriate: "The sight of our internal organs is denied us. To how many men is it given to look upon their own . . . hearts, and live? The hidden geography of the body is as Medusa's head— one glimpse of which would render blind the presumptuous eye."[14] Indeed, seeing your heart's true nature is alarming for everyone. After committing adultery, murder, lying to the nation, and prolonging repentance for over a year, King David, the man after God's own heart, goes to the centerpiece of Yom Kippur and writes, "The sacrifice God wants is a broken spirit. God, you will not reject a heart that is broken and sorry for sin" (Psalm 51:17 NCV). This kind of heart and spirit comes when we stop masquerading as people who only "think they might need" Jesus.

Jesus asks us to face the reality that we are incapable of fixing ourselves. Peter fully needed Jesus, but still disowned him. However, not for one moment did Jesus ever disown Peter. Jesus' focus was not on the nation of Israel, not on the thousands whom he had healed, fed, or restored, not on the world or the church at large, but on Peter as an individual. Because of this, the love of God captured Peter's heart. As author and spiritual director Fil Anderson says, "People who beam brightly the light of Jesus have gazed deeply into the darkness of their own broken existence."[15]

Have you come to the end of yourself? Have you realized that regardless of how "good" you think you are, Jesus' invitation to the broken, disappointed, and spiritually bankrupt to sit at his table is an invitation to you? Again, as Jesus taught, "Blessed are the poor in spirit" (Matthew 5:3).

Indeed, after Jesus faces the shame of the cross and grave and is resurrected from the dead, he appears to his disciples. At breakfast one morning, there is another exchange between Jesus and Peter. Only this time it is Jesus reinstating the Rock, Peter. Jesus asks Peter three times if he loves him, and Peter insists he does (John 21:15–17). Why ask three times? Was Jesus not convinced that Peter loved him? Did Jesus need assurance? No. Though Peter did not understand initially, Jesus was doing two things: First, he was giving Peter the opportunity to express the contrite, loving side of his heart. And second, he is showing us that no one, regardless of how vehement their denial of Jesus, is outside the bounds of his grace. In fact, such a person may be restored and mightily used by God. Here, we see Jesus making room to reverse the cursing denials of Peter's mouth only seventy-two hours earlier.

My friend Dustin Kensrue, front man for the band Thrice, captured the relief Peter must have felt in a song called "Words in the Water," which talks about a curse being lifted from his heart and beholding "a brilliant light in the dark."[16]

Peter is filled with confidence in Jesus' love. Later, at Pentecost, Peter doesn't shudder, fumble, or deny Jesus. No, he preaches with unprecedented boldness to the crowds. In the words of Dr. Selzer, "When the patient becomes the surgeon, he goes straight for the soul."[17]

This is the same Peter who rebuked Jesus (Mark 8:32), took his eyes off of Jesus (Matthew 14:30), and denied Jesus (Mark 14:66–72). If Jesus can love, forgive, restore, and empower this man, is there any reason why he cannot do the same for you and me?

The tenet of grace alone isn't some boring point of theology that means nothing. Do you acknowledge that the eternal God clothed himself in flesh out of love, came among us, taught us, bled for us, died for us, rose from the dead for us, and welcomes us into his kingdom simply out of grace? If you conclude that this is absolutely crazy, absolutely uncalled for, and totally foolish, even reckless, you truly understand the power of the gospel. You agree with the French Christians of Paris, who litter the streets with graffiti, *"L'amour de Dieu est folie!"* ("The love of God is folly!") as Brennan Manning reminded us on so many occasions every Easter.[18]

That God would love us is beyond comprehension, for he is under no obligation to love, pursue, forgive, or call us his sons and daughters. But he does.

When we recognize our brokenness and God's goodness, it is the difference between humming "Amazing Grace" and shouting it from our souls.

A Personal Account

Something profound in my own experience of following Jesus occurred when he saved me from merely studying him behind two-inch-thick glass—me dressed in a white coat, goggles, and a mask—and handling him as some sort of specimen to be dissected for the sake of more data reporting (preaching). I started understanding Jesus as a *person* who is to be loved and encountered. *That* is the best Christian theology has to offer, my friend. Not homework, but a conversation. Not a distant handshake, but a real embrace. Not a contract, but a covenant. We all know that blood is thicker than water, and that's exactly what this is about. Jesus is not in love with some future version of you or what you used to be. He loves you right where you are, sitting in that chair.

> **Jesus is not in love with some future version of you or what you used to be. He loves you right where you are.**

Personally, I have experienced the love of Jesus by the indwelling Holy Spirit not only on the mountaintops but also in the valleys of life. Did you know that Jesus not only suffers *for* you but also suffers *with* you? He shows compassion. This can be demonstrated fairly simply with basic exegesis. Our English version of the word *compassion* comes from the Latin, which literally means "to suffer with." At a scene of final judgment, Jesus says to those before him, "As you did it to one of the least of these my brothers, you did it to me" (Matthew 25:40). New Testament scholar and theologian R. T. France states, "Here his identification with his people goes further: *their experiences are his experiences, and what is done to them is done to him.*"[19] If you are his sheep, Jesus is part of your current sufferings.

Dietrich Bonhoeffer wrote, "God loves human beings. God loves the world. Not an ideal human, but human beings as they are; not an ideal world, but the real world. What we find repulsive in their opposition to God, what we shrink back from with pain and hostility, namely, real human beings, the real world, this is for God the ground of unfathomable love."[20]

He Wept With Me

Once a quarter, I take a couple of days to disconnect from the busyness of being a pastor and professor and retreat to a countryside monastery. I so look forward to these retreats where I can be alone for prayer and communion with Jesus. A few months ago, on August 4, I woke up on a rainy Wednesday morning after a good night's sleep. That date may not mean much to you, but it is extremely significant to me. You see, my dad passed away three years ago, totally unexpected, and August 4 is his birthday. If you've lost someone close to you, you know how hard birthdays, holidays, and other special occasions can be.

On my retreat that rainy morning, a worn tape started playing in my head, playing back moments of the day I learned my dad had died. I had been home alone, in my back office, studying for a sermon when I got the news and reality wrapped its icy fingers around me. I crumpled out of my chair, curled up under my desk, and wailed and wailed in total sadness, anger, and disbelief. I cried out to God the very question he asked in the garden of Eden, *Where are you?* "Christ, where are you?" I shouted. "Christ, where are you? Don't you see what's going on under your watch? I'm about to be a father, and you take mine away from me?" A sudden calm wrapped around me like a blanket. I knew Jesus was there. He had wept at Lazarus's graveside, and he was weeping with me. He was heartbroken with me over sin and its innumerably devastating effects. And, in that stillness, I simply knew that Jesus loved me deep in the valley of my heartache. You see, Christianity is not only for our mountaintops; our faith thrives in the valleys of life.

Perhaps you have some questions about this Jesus and his over-the-top love for you. Here's how I imagine a conversation going.

Jesus, you have no idea how bad I've been.

Yes I do. In fact, I expected worse out of you than you expected out of yourself.

Jesus, what if I don't ever get any better?

I'll always love you.

Jesus, what if I do it again?

We'll cross that bridge when we get there. I've got a plan.

Jesus, what if I just give up on you?

I'll never quit on you.

Jesus, how do you expect me to forgive _____ when they've been so hurtful to me?

Just give them what you get from me: grace. Just charge it to my account.

Jesus, but what about how insensitive they've been to me?

Charge that to my account too.

Jesus, I'm tired.

I'll be your rest.

Jesus, are you mad at me?

You're the apple of my eye—my beloved.

Jesus, what do you want me to do for you?

Don't be so quick to work for me. Everybody wants to work for me. I want you to know me and live in my love and acceptance of you.

Jesus, what if I fall asleep when I pray?
I'm happy you feel comfortable in my presence. Rest well.
I'll see you when you wake up.
Jesus, what if I don't understand all of the Bible?
I am the Word of the Word.
Jesus, I don't know where I belong.
You belong with me.
Jesus, what if I'm lazy?
You're not lazy. You're just distracted. We can change that.
Jesus, I'm mad.
I'll take your anger.
Jesus, I'm disappointed.
Keep looking at me.
Jesus, I'm sad.
I know. I see you right there. Want to talk to me about it?
Jesus, I'm drunk.
You're my friend.
Jesus, I stole.
I'll take care of it.
Jesus, I'm lustful.
Give me your heart.
Jesus, I hate myself.
My love for you will drown your hate of you.
Jesus, they told me I could lose my salvation. Is that true?
If you could lose it, don't you think you would've lost it
by now?
Jesus, I repent.
Let's get on to living now, shall we?

6

Jesus Loves Me
This I Know,
for the Bible Tells Me So

"I thank God for that word *whosoever*. If God had said there was mercy for Richard Baxter, I am so vile a sinner that I would have thought he meant some other Richard Baxter; but, when he says whosoever, I know that includes me, the worst of all Richard Baxters."[1]

—Richard Baxter (1615–1691)

"The poet only asks to get his head into the heavens. It is the logician who seeks to get the heavens into his head and it is his head that splits."[2]

—G. K. Chesterton

How can any of us truly know that Jesus actually loves us—especially given that we live in a culture in which love has become so transitory and so devalued? At one time, many people stood starry-eyed before the ones they loved and swore "until death do us part." Then a huge percentage of these people found themselves brutally arguing night after night, eventually culminating in standing before a judge and hiring moving trucks. One of my recently divorced friends described that day as pure hell. Another said it felt like drowning.

How do we know Jesus won't "file for divorce," especially when he sees how we *really* think and *really* feel so often? Or, consider the friends who promised that they've "got your back" and that "come hell or high water" they'll be loyal, only to discover that they didn't really have your back as much as they were watching it for the perfect time to insert their knife of betrayal. Is Jesus such a "friend"? If you're like me, you may leave church on Sunday morning convinced that he loves you and you are ready to walk on water. Then on Monday morning, you awaken doubting God's promises, questioning God's goodness, resisting surrender and those seven ever-so-risky words "Not my will but yours be done."

Jesus' love for us differs from any spouse or friend's love, and you can know this for certain—by faith. I know certainty and faith seem contradictory, but stick with me. These terms don't oppose one another as in a boxing contest, but complement one another like a nice filet and red wine. Let me emphasize that faith is a gift from God to an individual, and after God regenerates (imparts new life to) a person, he gives faith that leads to ongoing trust. However, this trust does not come easily to any of us, so this is simply a beckoning to whom and what we continue to place our faith in.

But let's move beyond traditional Christian thinking to consider why it is so hard for us to *know* that Jesus truly loves us.

The Secular and the Sacred

Christian subcultures removed from the outside world can create formidable obstacles to one's knowledge of God's love for the individual. It may feel nice to be in church gatherings "where everybody knows your name," like the TV bar *Cheers,* but that's not how the world is. When church gatherings and community groups are the only circles you run in, the likelihood of growing bored or sour in your faith goes up, not down.

When church gatherings and community groups are the only circles you run in, the likelihood of growing bored or sour in your faith goes up, not down.

God's salvation is not intended to be kept to ourselves but shared with the world. This means not just getting on an airplane every once in a while to serve in a foreign country for a week, but intentionally being a friend of sinners like Jesus did. Nothing will stoke the gospel fires of your heart like when you extend the grace of God to those who don't know him yet. It is a subtle deception that says, "If I hide out in my safe, polished little Christian community and avoid everyone who isn't like me, I'll be holy and happy." This could not be further from the truth. When we get out of our normal circles and listen to people's stories, sense the brokenness that exists within, and hear their questions, and then share with them the love and grace that God extends through Christ, it drastically affects how we think God feels about us personally. Writer Anne Lamott had a priest-friend tell her, "You can safely assume that you've created a God in your own image when it turns out that God hates all the same people you do."³

Certainly this was in the line of thinking of the apostle Paul when he spoke to the Philippian church. He said that he counted everything as rubbish compared to the intimate knowledge of Christ. Prior to that, he made it clear that he wanted to depart and be with Christ in heaven: "For to me to live is Christ, and to die is gain." But then he said, "If I am to live in the flesh, that means fruitful labor for me" (Philippians 1:21–22). Part of this fruitful labor certainly included the very preaching of the gospel to those who did not know it yet. Consider, too, how he speaks to Timothy: "I endure everything for the sake of the elect, that they also may obtain the salvation that is in Christ Jesus with eternal glory" (2 Timothy 2:10). The sufferings were immense:

. . . imprisonments, with countless beatings, and often near death. Five times I received at the hands of the Jews the forty lashes less one. Three times I was beaten with rods. Once I was stoned. Three times I was shipwrecked; a night and a day I was adrift at sea; on frequent journeys, in danger from rivers, danger from robbers, danger from my own people, danger from Gentiles, danger in the city, danger in the wilderness, danger at sea, danger from false brothers; in toil and hardship, through many a sleepless night, in hunger and thirst, often without food, in cold and exposure. And, apart from other things, there is the daily pressure on me of my anxiety for all the churches.

2 Corinthians 11:23–28

The Night Before You Met Jesus

Telling others about the love of Jesus has a way of carving deep grooves in your heart. Truly, just think about where you were, who you were with, and what you loved *the night before* you met Jesus. Did you put your head on the pillow at night when the phone was hung up, the music and television turned off, and it was just you and your thoughts? Did you feel the loneliness that accompanies a self-sufficient "I don't need God" approach to life? Did you have questions like *What in the world am I doing here on earth?* or *What's the point of all of this?* That's where countless people in your city, your neighborhood, your workplace, are every single day. The great hymn "Amazing Grace" captures this moment perfectly: *How precious did that grace appear the hour I first believed!*[4]

Do you remember that hour? Revisit it often.

> **Telling others about the love of Jesus has a way of carving deep grooves in your heart.**

Two Cultures

As I mentioned, I'm from Georgia, but I've also had the opportunity to live in London, Seattle, and Reno, Nevada. No matter the setting, I've seen churchgoers live in two cultures

121

and unknowingly hold what I call a pseudo-Christian-dualistic worldview. It works like this: We have the secular and the sacred, the profane and the holy—the private life we don't want anyone to know about and the public life we want everyone to see. Attending church, religious events, Bible reading, and the like belong to the sacred; while everything, everyone, and every other place outside of the church building or Christian gatherings are considered "secular."

Some of this stems from our education. Starting in public elementary school, many are taught an atheistic approach to the really big questions of life such as "How did we get here?" and "Who is responsible for everything I can see, taste, touch, smell, and hear?" As a nine-year-old, I learned that given a significant amount of time, plus enough matter, plus chance, equals the precise formula needed to trigger a cosmic explosion, thus resulting in all existence, including human life.

During the latter part of the nineteenth century, with Darwinian thought increasingly pervasive, writers such as Friedrich Nietzsche (1844–1900) exalted the notion of the "superman" and proclaimed the "death" of God, hoping to free mankind from moral obligations to God and questioning putting one's trust in Scripture. While Nietzsche's works may not have been read by many in the Bible Belt or by many of my teachers, his ideas had momentous consequences. As a child, I learned on Sundays that God is not dead but living, and he alone is responsible for bringing everything and everyone into existence. I also learned about sin, Jesus' cross, and a new heaven and new earth in which evil would be banished. Then, paradoxically, on Monday through Friday at school,

I learned, at least implicitly, that God is dead and that I and everything else can trace our origins to nothing, that good and bad are relative, and that none of us will ultimately answer to anyone for our good or bad deeds.

My individual childhood experiences of this sacred/secular divide could be multiplied countless times. Since I have become a pastor and church planter, I've noticed that, though separated by two thousand years, five thousand miles, and the enormous barriers created by language, diet, social customs, and theologies, Evangelicalism and the first-century Galilean home of Jesus have some things in common regarding the sacred and secular divide. The figure below demonstrates my point:

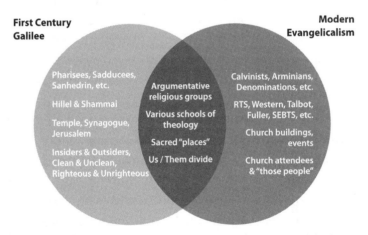

First Century Galilee

Modern Evangelicalism

Pharisees, Sadducees, Sanhedrin, etc.

Hillel & Shammai

Temple, Synagogue, Jerusalem

Insiders & Outsiders, Clean & Unclean, Righteous & Unrighteous

Argumentative religious groups

Various schools of theology

Sacred "places"

Us / Them divide

Calvinists, Arminians, Denominations, etc.

RTS, Western, Talbot, Fuller, SEBTS, etc.

Church buildings, events

Church attendees & "those people"

Same: Steeped in moralism, outward piety, fear of man, justified by works

Today's evangelical church hasn't helped the problem. In fact, it often compounds the fracture by ostracizing everything and everyone that doesn't fit the Awana (or other comparable) box. Ask your average bartender why he doesn't go to church, and he'll tell you he tried going to church, but felt ostracized. Christians ought to be careful not to rashly conclude that such an individual "couldn't deal with the truth." Sadly, many widows, single moms, those out of work, you name it, have never heard the truth of the reckless love of God because the church stereotypes or rejects them before they even walk through the door. The church of today is not far from the days of Salem. In many places, churches will happily supply the wood, the stake, and the fire for the "witches" of postmodernity. Unfortunately, much of the evangelical church can be defined more by what it is *against* than by what it is *for*.

Indeed, there are evangelicals who are against Disney, rap, heavy metal, off-color movies, the scientific community specifically, and intellectuals in general. Putting their heads in the sand, such evangelicals often profess a blind, naïve optimism with heavy doses of "don't taste, don't touch, don't smell," which supposedly passes for holiness or Christlikeness. Sadly, these individuals demonstrate a bunker mentality, confining themselves within the walls of their churches, while rarely using their minds to engage cultural manifestations and ask substantive questions. Within such sterile worlds, individuals, in the name of maintaining harmony in the body, dare not ask questions, dare not rock the boat, stay quiet, drink the juice (not the wine!), and appear, at least superficially, as "good." Certainly, Jesus did not come

Jesus did not come to make a few minor adjustments to people's morality. He came to turn the world upside down.

to make a few minor adjustments to people's morality. He came to turn the world upside down.

Living in this dual world of "us versus them" has harmed and weakened the evangelical church and helped nurture immoral moralists who have often prompted a lost world to ignore Jesus and to dismiss Scripture and its claims. Secularism, atheism, and moralism create comparable problems. In the end, we are left struggling to pull ourselves up by our bootstraps—either in the name of the survival of the fittest, the name of the greatest good for the greatest number, or the name of earning God's love.

The Route of Faith

What am I suggesting? I'm saying that a way to live that dwarfs both secularism and moralism is by *faith* in the person and work of Jesus Christ. Both Christians and unbelievers need to remember that faith is not something for the gullible, simple, blind, naïve individual who, while emotionally crippled, needs a "crutch" to cope with life. Real faith is bold and far from trivial.

God isn't intimidated by our questions or doubts. In fact, he gave us our minds and welcomes our questions. Even while on earth, Jesus expected his critics to examine his words and his works, to test them, and to authentically trust that he is who he says he is and will do precisely what he says he will do (John 10:37–38). Professor Andrew Latz of Durham University says, "Jesus asks that people give the evidence a fair hearing, that they honestly examine his claim to work and speak for the Father [cf. John 9: 1–41]. He coerces no one into belief in himself."[5]

In urging people to have faith in Jesus alone, I don't want to patronize them by saying, "Just believe this message, because I say so," and be met with glazed-over eyes, a shrug of the shoulders, and a response of "Fine. I'll comply." God gave you and me incredible minds, and the gospel isn't grasped with a "whatever" shrug of the shoulders. Rather, when embraced, the gospel causes a thoughtful, calculated, reckless, joyful abandonment that becomes the all-consuming message, theme, and purpose of our lives (Matthew 13:44). Anything less is simply *not* the gospel.

Even more, I don't want to patronize Jesus. He gave everything so that we would surrender ourselves and place our faith in him. The Bible says that Jesus was born to the Virgin Mary and her husband, Joseph, in a barn (Luke 2:7), and because his life was in immediate danger, he was smuggled out of the country (Matthew 2:13). Years later, he returned with his family to Israel. Jesus lived a sinless life (Hebrews 4:15), performed miracles before both believers and nonbelievers, was tried by the state (Luke 23:1–15), executed (Luke 23:46), rose from the dead (Mark 16:6), appeared to hundreds of eyewitnesses (1 Corinthians 15:6), and ascended back into heaven, promising to build rooms for his people; then returning to take them to be with him forever (Acts 1:9–11; John 14:1–3). Such demonstrates that the Jesus of Scripture is not glorified by our rejecting reason and grudgingly going along with this whole "Christian charade."

Every one of us who calls ourselves Christian struggles with the "this I *know*" part of living out our faith. Here's how I know that you struggle with what you know: You're a human being. As a Christian, though redeemed, there's more work to be done. God, speaking through the apostle Paul, says,

> God chose the foolish things of the world to shame the wise;
> God chose the weak things of the world to shame the strong.
> God chose the lowly things of this world and the despised
> things—and the things that are not—to nullify the things
> that are.
>
> 1 Corinthians 1:27–28 NIV

We are told elsewhere to renew our minds (Romans 12:2). This is what Jesus people *have* to do—engage in daily renewal. So this means that if you spend fifty years of your life as a Christian, you will see 18,262 sunrises and sunsets during which you are expected to renew your mind as you journey toward heaven. We all struggle, but having faith that Jesus loves us, we can trust that he will carry us through these days that are not ours to control.

Three of the Biggest Obstacles

I have professed to be a Christian for nineteen years, but it is only in the last five years that I've been able to really *know* that Jesus loves me—not just in a theological sense. Countless other factors affected my acceptance that Jesus really does *love me*! Here are three; then we'll seal the deal.

Projection

French mathematician, physicist, and religious philosopher Blaise Pascal (1623–1662) wrote, "God made man in his own image and man returned the compliment."[6] If there is one thing that has consistently slowed my spiritual growth, it is this: I think Jesus loves me only when I'm good and when I do the things I should do.

I would say that for the majority of my Christian life, I have projected onto Jesus a type of love that resembles mine: weak, fickle, transient, manipulative, able and willing to be bribed, stubborn, and most certainly conditional. If I'm honest, my expression of love has been far from steadfast; instead, I've possessed the what's-in-it-for-me gene for a long time. So when it comes to knowing whether Jesus loves me, I really couldn't say for sure, because if he's the way I project, then he would give up on me or, at best, leave me in a constant state of questioning whether his love persists. Maybe we have this in common. However, such is not the truth.

> **Projecting our notions of conditional, what's-in-it-for-me love is one way to forget that Jesus loves and knows each of us.**

If Jesus were looking at you eye to eye today, based on how he has revealed himself in Scripture, I believe that he would say, "My beloved, do not for one moment be so brash as to mistake my divine, untainted, scandalous love for yours. My love doesn't waver with every new impulse or fad. I am totally self-sufficient, and I still want *you*! I really do have it all together. I am the definition and the personification of love. Come to me. You can trust me." So, projecting our notions of conditional, what's-in-it-for-me love is one way to forget that Jesus loves and knows each of us as an individual.

Inoculation

Another problem is Satan's subtle tactic of inoculation. Inoculation works like this: A doctor takes a small amount of a virus and injects it into your bloodstream so that your immune system will naturally kick in, do battle, and counter it—thus building up an immunity to the virus, so that if the virus strikes naturally, your body can throw it off. Figuratively, inoculation also operates with many believers in many churches. For example, we often get just snippets of the gospel and so become immune to the power of the gospel. How does this happen? Well, many of us go to church Sunday after Sunday, out of habit, with no intention of actually becoming like Jesus, dealing with sin, or decreasing so that he might increase. There's a comfortable way to go about discipleship, or so we think. We church folk even have our own language we call "Christianese." Christians use words or phrases that simply have zero relevance to those who don't know or run in our circles. For example, *born again, washed in the blood of the Lamb, backsliding,* and so on. Of course, "Christianese" is part of this inoculation as individuals talk the missional game, blog about it, tweet about it, read about it, go to conferences dedicated to it, but never actually *do it!*

You see, one way to escape knowing that Jesus really loves us is by choosing to avoid becoming friends with sinners, thereby missing the privilege of seeing him work through the Holy Spirit in other people's lives. Sadly, I'm quite serious. One way that I saw this was that I lived in a Christian subculture without even knowing it, and subsequently became less like the Jesus who found me bound up in sin. Jesus came to do anything but maintain boring, predictable, religious behavior that keeps the outsiders outside. His practice of sharing meals with blatant sinners was considered so scandalous that it infuriated more than just a few people.

Hans Kung, a Swiss Catholic theologian and prolific writer, born in 1928, said that Jesus' "problem" was "that he got involved with *moral failures*, with obviously *irreligious* and *immoral people:* people morally and politically suspect, so many dubious, obscure, abandoned, hopeless types, on the fringe of every society. This was the real scandal. Did he really have to go so far?"[7]

I had removed myself from the rest of the world that used four-letter words, hung around with "that crowd," listened to "objectionable" music on the radio, watched "offensive" movies, read non-prescribed literature, etc. I had exchanged the amazing life of sharing the good news of the gospel with the very people Jesus would befriend for Christian busyness, activities, and a polished little religious résumé. In Jesus' name, I was not a friend of sinners because, after all, I'm supposed to live "in the world and not be of it," right? I realized, though, that this verse means not capitulating to what the world loves, pursuing what the world pursues, and glorying in what the world esteems. I could still engage with, listen to, and love fellow sinners who very much lived in this same world.

How did I get so far off? Quite simply, my fear of a religious subculture and of men with titles and often well-published opinions dwarfed my fear of God and love for those whom Jesus came to save. The Bible's demand that I actually care about the lost shrunk to a rote mumbled prayer every once in a while: *Dear God, only you can help that guy. Look at him. Please send along a Christian to invite him to church sometime. Amen.*

Isolation Leads to Inoculation

It's easy to pull this off in the pop-evangelical culture. It's not only possible, but even probable, for many to grow up in a Christian home, attend a Christian college, meet a Christian girl or guy, have a Christian wedding, get a job at a Christian church or business, hang out only with Christian friends (calling it "community"), go to Christian restaurants, go on Christian cruises, play Christian sports at our Christian life centers, watch Christian TV programs and movies, play Christian video games, read Christian magazines and books, listen to Christian music, wear Christian T-shirts, enjoy Christian breath mints, download Christian ring tones, wear Christian bracelets, drop your kids off at Christian daycare or private Christian school. Such, no doubt, is a hermetically sealed, inoculated environment.

In fact, you can even become a professional Christian conference-goer, wearing the right clothes, dropping in on only the sessions that "matter," and being seen in the right places at the right times with the right people. Once you spend enough time being inoculated to the gospel and keeping your hands clean within the confines of a church's walls, it's easy to reduce Jesus' ferocious love and reckless message of the gospel of grace to nothing more than systematics, semantics, and a system to study. You might even go to seminary, write some books, plant a church, and develop some systems for discipleship. All this is possible and yet you might still have a heart unmoved by the gospel. When this happens, genuine knowledge of his relentless, incessant, unremitting, aggressive love for you will inevitably fade, grow dull, and deteriorate in the name of disconnected, whitewashed religion. In this environment, the Lion appears tame, toothless, and harmless. His nails are trimmed, his mane is brushed, and he's well-mannered. He looks like he belongs in a petting zoo, placed to turn tricks for those who walk by, patting his head and saying, "Yes, he's cute. What's next?"

It's easy to reduce Jesus' ferocious love and reckless message of the gospel of grace to nothing more than systematics, semantics, and a system to study.

This Jesus becomes a homework assignment, taskmaster, or dull employer when he is caged in and relegated to weekend retreats for people who already claim to know him, or by the "experts" who assign him a seat at the "Do this in remembrance of me" table but never allow him to stand up. No, he must remain confined in the church building until the following Sunday, because he's certainly no match for the filthy city streets of North America and the United Kingdom. After all, these streets abound in drunkards, gluttons, prostitutes, the homeless, jobless outcasts. So church often becomes a sterile, monastic prison that fails to engage the lost, broken, confused, and skeptical people of this world—the very opposite of what Jesus, the friend of sinners, came to do!

If one hangs out in such a church long enough, the song ends up sounding like this: "Jesus loves me, this I *hope*." The reason I say "this I hope" is because this sort of Christian practice is handicapped; the practitioners don't actually *see* Jesus in action by loving other sinners. Instead, Jesus resembles a venerable grandfather, whose glory days have ended. When we've reduced the gospel and followed these practices long enough, why should Jesus' love be real to us? You see, mission and the knowledge of the gospel that Jesus loves us cannot be separated.

Unrepentant Sin

Finally, another way that we, and many other Christians, have lost confidence in Jesus' love for us is persisting in unrepentant sin. Playing the blame game, ignoring sin, or denying sin committed by us or against us, totally frustrates the "abiding" that Jesus called us to, and it sends us packing our bags and moving into a halfway house or $50-a-week-stay-lodges known as "Christian camps" or "retreats." Going this route can cause our hearts to grow hard, our minds to become dull, and the Holy Spirit to grieve. We travel down a wide, smooth path and lose the knowledge of Jesus' love.

One example of unrepentant sin is the account in Second Samuel of David and Bathsheba. While David was supposed to be at war, he plays hooky and ends up sleeping with Uriah's wife, Bathsheba. Then David brings Uriah home from the battlefield, gets him drunk, and then sends him home, hoping that he will sleep with his wife. Then, David imagines, he'd be off the hook, because the child Bathsheba has conceived would be considered Uriah's, not his. Uriah upsets this plan because, as a faithful soldier, he remains loyal to his king rather than going home to his wife.

Rather than coming clean, David searches for more fig leaves to cover his shame—deciding to have Uriah placed on the front lines of the battlefield, and thus killed. A year passes. The baby is born, and soon dies. God, the eyewitness to all of David's sins, sends the prophet Nathan to David's door.

Nathan tells David a scandalous parable that robs David of his cover. He is busted, naked, and ashamed. Not long after, David wrote two songs (Psalms 32 and 51), thinking about the previous fifty-two weeks of lying that bound him in his own personal hell. He writes, "I said not a word, but my bones wasted away from groaning all the day" (Psalm 32:4 NJB). Such is what carrying around unrepentant sin feels like—bones rotting from within.

His Love Displayed

David's repentance restores his heart and his desire to dwell in God's love. Likewise, Jesus says something to his disciples at his last supper with them. He was soon to depart to build a home for them in heaven, but he wasn't leaving them entirely. He intended for them (and for us) to do something. John 15:9 records his saying: "As the Father has loved me, so have I loved you. Abide in my love." The word for "abide" here in Greek is *meno*. It means to indwell or build a home. Though he will be leaving, he desires for them to become completely familiar with and uncomfortably comfortable in his love. The next morning, Jesus himself provides the largest exclamation point in the history of the world, showing his earth-shattering love that transcends all other loves.

Knowledge of Jesus' love for you as an individual is not grounded only in the teachings and miracles of Jesus, or in the church, nor is it limited solely to the person and work of the Holy Spirit. Evidence of Jesus' love is ultimately grounded in one specific event in the Bible that encompasses every single letter, verse, jot, and tittle. Of course, I am speaking of the cross of Jesus. This single event grounds our knowledge of Jesus' love in something outside our wishy-washy, moody, flaky, sinful selves. At the cross, God demonstrates his own love, for "while we were still sinners, Christ died for us" (Romans 5:8). The cross is God's glorifying rescue mission that says, "Since you cannot and will not come to me, I am coming to you because I *love you*!" The cross gives us an objective event that paints the love of Jesus so that the brightest colors imaginable sear our dull minds and hard hearts.

> **The cross is God's glorifying rescue mission that says, "Since you cannot and will not come to me, I am coming to you because I love you!"**

Having faith in Jesus alone is saying that not only does a Christian have faith in who God says he is but he also has faith in what God accomplished through the cross of Jesus. Reformer Martin Luther said, "This doctrine is the head and cornerstone. It alone begets, nourishes, builds, preserves, and defends the church of God; and without it the church of God cannot exist for one hour."[8]

Recently, it has become increasingly popular for some theologians, teachers, and authors to question and openly deny one aspect of Jesus' work on the cross due to the "problems" they perceive it creates. This aspect is the doctrine of penal substitutionary atonement. This doctrine means that God the Father, perfectly holy and just, pours out all of his wrath and hatred for sin on his Son, Jesus, rather than on us as individuals. Thus Jesus dies *for* all of our sins (1 Corinthians 15:3).

Liberal scholar Rudolph Bultmann writes, "What a primitive mythology it is that a divine being should become incarnate, and atone for the sins of men through his own blood."[9] Others echo Bultmann's ideas. In their book, *Christianity, Patriarchy, and Abuse: A Feminist Critique*, Joanne Brown and Rebecca Parker state in their chapter "For God So Loved the World?":

> Is it any wonder that there is so much abuse in the modern society when the predominant image of the culture is of "divine child abuse"—God the Father demanding and carrying out the suffering death of his own son? If Christianity is to be liberating for the oppressed, it must itself be liberated from this theology. We must do away with the atonement, this idea of a blood sin upon the whole human race which can be washed away only by the blood of the lamb.[10]

Other popular writers and activists, such as Steve Chalke, Brian McLaren, and Rob Bell have followed suit. These and many others are frustrated by God's holiness, his anger over sin, and the justice of penalizing his Son. However, their arguments result only in reducing God to something after their own image, while contradicting Scripture. If God doesn't pour out wrath on Jesus, then the Old Testament promise "The soul who sins shall die" (Ezekiel 18:20) along with over six hundred verses revealing God's anger over sin are reduced to mere bluffs, elementary rhetoric, and empty threats to prod people toward making the right decision. Our God is holy. "This is what sends hearts into throats and turns knees to jelly."[11] The words of Scripture cause us to gulp and get weak in the knees, and being made uncomfortable is one of God's ways of loving us best. Nigel Wright, principal of Spurgeon's College in London, states, "The demands of moral theology compel the church to condemn sin. The demands of pastoral theology compel the church to love sinners. When the church condemns sin she is accused of not caring for sinners. When she cares for sinners she is accused of being soft on sin."[12]

This is a far bigger problem because it doesn't square with the God revealed in the Bible, who hates sin and will not be mocked by his creation. This articulation of the gospel is grounded in what the New Testament apostles make abundantly clear, as we will see. Karl Barth (1886–1968), the Swiss reformed theologian, attests to the truth of this when he wrote of Jesus' death: "The Judge [has been] judged in our place."[13] The anvil of God's justice fell on Jesus Christ. Not on me. Not on you.

Christ and His Broken Heart

Regardless of the context or situation, it is fundamentally impossible to speak of the love of Jesus and knowledge of this love divorced from the cross and its implications. If you would have asked any of the apostles on any given day, they would have consistently returned to the cross. It didn't matter if they were in jail or standing before kings, their focus remained on Jesus' cross—the perspective from which they invariably viewed the world and everything in

It is fundamentally impossible to speak of the love of Jesus and knowledge of this love divorced from the cross and its implications.

it. The cross alone provides answers to questions posited throughout history by Marxism, Nihilism, Socialism, Existentialism, and other *isms*.

Have you ever considered that the primary symbol of the Christian faith, the cross, is one of shame and disgrace, not power and authority? Christianity's symbol could have easily been the manger or an empty tomb. But manger scenes at Christmastime hardly cause anyone to shudder, for, after all, Jesus is still only a baby to some. The empty tomb may be wrongly interpreted by others as a symbol of escaping from the present evil age. The symbol of the cross, however, speaks precisely to the world as it is.

Boldly and courageously, Martin Luther countered argument after argument posed by the Catholic Church in the sixteenth century, finally exclaiming, *"Crux sola est nostra theologia!"* Luther proclaimed, "The cross alone is our theology!" Luther helps us see that God is totally concealed, for how could God have anything to do with the disgusting mess created through the scourging, taunting, and torturing of a man charged with criminal blasphemy? In addition, Luther shows that God is totally revealed for the centurion who crucified Jesus, for his mother Mary, for his beloved disciple John, and millions of others who later found God to be totally present in what appeared to be the abandonment of his only begotten Son. We see that in the hours following Jesus' asking his Abba why he has been forsaken, he then, on his way to unconsciousness and death, manifests unflinching trust, unbroken communion, and confident prayer, saying, "Father, into your hands I commit my spirit." Princeton theologian B. B. Warfield said,

In the presence of this mental anguish, the physical tortures of the crucifixion retire into the background, and we may well believe that our Lord, though he died on the cross, yet died not *of* the cross, but, as we commonly say, of a broken heart, that is to say, the strain of his mental suffering.[14]

The cross remains remarkable for those of us who know Jesus because his cross was totally unnecessary. Jesus was not obligated to love us, save us, leave heaven and pay the price for our sins, to crush the works and effects of Satan, and to erase every time we were the culprit or the victim. Jesus' cross was not a passive death like that of a sacrificial animal. Rather, Jesus' death was the single most voluntary, self-willed act of outrageous love in the history of the universe!

The Attempt to Make Jesus Forgotten

A few years ago, my wife and I enjoyed realizing a dream. As I mentioned earlier, we moved to London, England, so that I could go to the London School of Theology. Though frequenting Hyde Park, Leicester Square, Covent Garden, and Portobello Market was delightful, I spent most of my days in the back of the library, in the periodicals room, reading journal articles in my carrel or tucked away upstairs in the annex studying the cross of Jesus. All of my classes were held in the Guthrie Research Center, named for the English professor and scholar now gone to heaven, Donald Guthrie. On one occasion, he wrote of the cross of Jesus: "The voluntary act was not in the interest of personal heroism, but because of dynamic love. He knew that it was for this purpose he had come into the world."[15]

The earliest Christians recognized Christ's humility and love by writing a hymn that was quoted by the apostle Paul to the church in Philippi:

> Have this mind among yourselves, which is yours in Christ Jesus, who, though he was in the form of God, did not count equality with God a thing to be grasped, but emptied himself, by taking the form of a servant, being born in the likeness of men. And being found in human form, he humbled himself by becoming obedient to the point of death, even death on a cross. Therefore God has highly exalted him and bestowed on him the name that is above every name, so that at the name of Jesus every knee should bow, in heaven and on earth and under the earth, and every tongue confess that Jesus Christ is Lord, to the glory of God the Father.
>
> Philippians 2:5–11

Jesus' entire earthly ministry, beginning with his descent through Mary's womb to the cross that he wasn't strong enough to carry, to burial in a borrowed grave, was what Greek Christians referred to as his *kenosis*—literally his self-emptying. Jesus was not tipped over; he poured himself out. Those who crucified Jesus did not desire his fame. They didn't imagine the world being turned upside down or anything of this nature (Acts 17:6). No, they hoped to erase him from history for good. Scholar and professor of the New Testament at St. Andrews in Aberdeen, Scotland, Richard Bauckham, writes:

> Crucifixion was the way of removing them [criminals], rendering them nothing; and so they might be well and truly *forgotten*, crucifixion itself was not discussed [among civilians].[16]

Christians continue to experience this dark reality when we observe Holy Communion, attend Good Friday services, and meditate on the cross. The evangelist Luke records that during Jesus' death "the sun's light failed" (Luke 23:45). How ironic that the light of the world, shrouded in our spiritual darkness and sin would also die in "failing sunlight." This prompts the question: "Who in the world voluntarily dies alone, in the dark, to save a rebel?" The only answer is Jesus, who was driven by his desire to proclaim God's glory and manifest his love for his people.

Jesus' beloved disciple John wrote boldly and frequently of Jesus' love. In AD 80, in the region of Turkey, he wrote: "By this we know love, that he laid down his life for us, and we ought to lay down our lives for the brothers" (1 John 3:16). The original word for "know" in this verse is *egnokamen*, and it refers to a knowledge that is gained by diligent contemplation. The word *know* here is in the perfect tense, which refers to a completed action—in this case, a historical encounter with Jesus that has ongoing implications in daily life. John's point is that the way to know love is to determine whether or not it is ongoing. For a Christian, such love entails a daily gazing at the cross of Jesus, where his love was so boldly demonstrated.

You might be wondering, *What about me? Surely God has given up on me by now.* If you return to the cross of Jesus, and see it for what it truly is, can you still conclude that you have gone too far? John continues in 1 John 4:10: "This is love: not that we loved God, but that he loved us and sent

141

his Son as an atoning sacrifice for our sins" NIV). John pre-emptively strikes against our pride. He reveals what Jesus called the "secrets of the kingdom of heaven" and tells us that we didn't love God first, so that he would then love us. Rather, it was quite the opposite. Whatever love you have for God derives from his love for you. He made the first move. Yes, we may have loved things *about* God—but not *God* himself! We may love the gifts of God—but not God the Giver! We may have loved aspects of creation—but not God as Creator! And yet, despite our feeble attempts and our sin, Jesus left heaven and became the *hilasmos*, the propitiation, for us. Jesus became the wrath-bearing sacrifice for our sins and cleanses us from all unrighteous-ness. This is perfect love—Jesus, the penalty and substitute for our sins!

Scripture repeatedly proclaims and celebrates Jesus' love:

- "Greater love has no one than this, that someone lay down his life for his friends" (John 15:13).
- "For God so loved the world, that he gave his only Son, that whoever believes in him should not perish but have eternal life" (John 3:16).
- "And walk in love, as Christ loved us and gave him-self up for us, a fragrant offering and sacrifice to God" (Ephesians 5:2).
- "Christ redeemed us from the curse of the law by be-coming a curse for us—for it is written, 'Cursed is everyone who is hanged on a tree'" (Galatians 3:13).
- "Husbands, love your wives, as Christ loved the church and gave himself up for her" (Ephesians 5:25).

He Lived for Me! He Died for Me!

Such verses objectively declare that Jesus loves you and proved it by dying your death, in your place, and giving you his righteousness to go before God completely spotless both now and forever. As a Christian today, you will never be more justified before God than you are right now. You will never be more forgiven than you are right now. You will never be more accepted than you are right now. God is just, and he is the justifier! Pastor and scholar R. C. Sproul writes, "By his sinless life he achieved positive merit, which merit is imputed to all who put their faith in him. Christ not only died for us, he lived for us as well."[17]

Repeatedly, the New Testament speaks to the fact that I can know Jesus loves me not only objectively, through looking at the cross, but also *subjectively* based on my experience of (or through) the cross in my daily life as a believer filled with the Holy Spirit. Here is commentary from a Bible scholar on Galatians 2:20:

> "I have been crucified with Christ. It is no longer I who live, but Christ who lives in me. And the life I now live in the flesh I live by faith in the Son of God, who loved me and gave himself for me."

> Paul sees this love as extending to all Christians, but the individualistic emphasis must not be neglected. Faith in Christ can be sustained only where one is confident of God's love. Love, in this sense, is the fuel of faith.[18]

Now let's read this verse a bit differently. Remove Paul's personal pronouns, and in your poverty of spirit and with the bold confidence you have in the person and work of Jesus, put your name in the blanks:

"_____ [has] been crucified with Christ. It is no longer _____ who [lives], but Christ who lives in _____. And the life _____ now [lives] in the flesh _____ [lives] by faith in the Son of God, who loved _____ and gave himself for _____."

Let me conclude by asking some questions:

- Do you need more evidence than the cross that Jesus loves you?
- How central is the cross in your view of Christianity?
- Are you struggling with knowing because you've become inoculated to the gospel?
- Do you have unrepentant sin that distorts your thinking?
- Do you project your ideas of love onto Jesus rather than having him inform yours?
- Have you savored the power of the cross to stay reminded of his love?
- Are you convinced that he will never leave you or forsake you?

As you conclude this chapter, prayerfully reflect upon these questions. Through the power of the Holy Spirit, Jesus' perfect love (*yes*, he most certainly *does* love you!) and his merciful grace are abundantly present to touch and change your heart and your life.

7

Jesus Loves Me This I Know, for the Bible Tells Me So

"God has shown me that he loves me in that while I was yet a sinner, Christ died for me (Romans 5:8). This is not faith in history; it is not faith in the kerygma; it is not faith in the Bible. It is faith in God who has revealed himself to me in the historical event of the person, works, and words of Jesus of Nazareth who continues to speak to me through the prophetic word of the Bible."[1]

—George Eldon Ladd

Voltaire (1694–1778), a key figure in the French Enlightenment and the author of many works, including *Candide,* wrote, "Another century and there will not be another Bible on the earth!" Ironically, his house later became the headquarters for the Bible Society that printed and distributed thousands of Bibles.[2]

But *who* is the Bible about? Its diversity often leads people to conclude different things. Consider that it is comprised of sixty-six books, with over forty authors written more than four thousand years ago, in three languages. The cultural, theological, and philosophical differences provide more than enough distance between then and now. Many Christians don't know that those who finished compiling all of the New Testament letters had the entire Bible arranged according to different types or genres. Thus the Bible resembles a contemporary bookstore with books sorted according to stories/literature, poetry, history, biography, fiction, and so forth. The Bible includes law, prophets, wisdom literature, love poetry, gospels, history, and apocalyptic literature. During the Middle Ages, portions were numbered to facilitate quick reference, and these add up to 31,173 individual verses. Contributors to the Bible were not restricted by race, gender, or socioeconomic class. Men, women, doctors, lawyers, slaves, freemen, fishermen, young and old, rich and poor, kings and peasants, all played a significant role in writing the revelation of God that is the Bible.

> **The primary focus of the Bible is to reveal the glory of God on display in the person and work of Jesus.**

The primary focus of the Bible is to reveal the glory of God on display in the person and work of Jesus. But the Bible isn't the only book that talks about

Jesus. It is surprising to many to discover that more books have been written about Jesus than any other figure in world history. Author Stephen Prothero undertook the task of investigating how Jesus is understood and then morphed into various contexts throughout the world with a focus on North America. He writes,

> The Library of Congress holds more books about Jesus (seventeen thousand or so) than about any other historical figure, roughly twice as many as the runner-up (Shakespeare), and Jesus books there are piling up fast.[3]

Even other religious faiths, such as Islam and Buddhism, quote, cite, or borrow from Jesus, but he stands alone: He never returns this compliment. He is his own footnote. He did not draw from another source. He arrived as the long-awaited Messiah and the center of the content of the preaching of the apostles. He came to show us that truth is more than an idea or a concept. Rather, he came to show us that truth is bound up in his very identity.

Distinguished New Testament scholar Everett Ferguson writes,

> The truth claims of Christianity are bound up with the "person and work" of Jesus, who he was and what he did. What would make Christianity unique in an absolute sense, with no possible historical rival, would be for Jesus to be what is claimed for him—the one and only Son of God, God who has come in the flesh; and to have done what is affirmed for him—to have brought a salvation and relationship with God that no one else than the Son of God could have brought. There we pass from history to faith.[4]

It's All in the Approach

Given the diversity of both the text of Scripture and the various contexts it is read in today, there is most certainly a right and wrong way to go about reading the Bible. You can either read it as "This is what you must *do* in order to *earn* the love of God," or "This is what has been *done for you* by the love of God." Each approach to reading has massive consequences and will determine everything about your understanding of the Bible's message and your subsequent walk with God.

How you view God and understand yourself and your relationship with him and others in this world is of utmost importance. If you think the message of Scripture is telling you to get better, try harder, do more, and get on the hamster wheel of religious performance in order to show God that you're worthy of his love, you are bound to relate to God as a dictator. Jesus will be a cop that you avoid, and the church will be a community of people you find yourself competing with. However, if you think the Bible is God's revelation of his love for you, through no good works or super spirituality on your own, then you will relate to God as your Abba Father. Jesus will be a drink of cool water, and the church will be a community that you enjoy being around as you celebrate others. One approach results in relating to God as a stingy employer who seeks to squeeze every last penny out of your workday, despises giving bonuses, and most certainly doesn't care about you or your family. The other approach results in having a loving Father that you enjoy the privilege of knowing and being known by, who spoils you with the grace, love, and affection that you've always wanted, and keeps no record of wrongs.

The reckless love of God for you is not found on just one page, but *every* page of the Bible. This changes how we read it from cover to cover. If your starting point is with anything other than the nature of who God is and the reckless love he feels and demonstrates for you, then you're bound to end up missing the overall point of Scripture—that our holy, righteous, all-powerful God has gone to great lengths to forgive our sin, heal what is broken in us, and fill us with his eternal, unbreakable love.

The Bible Has Only One Hero

Many think the Bible is a big book with a lot of heroes, and that we are to conclude at the end of each story that we need to just try a little harder to be like so and so. However, when you look closer at the "heroes" of Scripture, you quickly discover that they're not really all that flawless. In fact, they're just as messed up as you and I are. For example, creation's first man, Adam, stood and watched while the talking serpent deceived his wife, Eve, and ruined human history. Father Abraham gave away his wife on at least two occasions. Noah got drunk and passed out in front of his sons. Moses was a murderer on the run from God and seemed to consistently wrestle with a significant temper problem. David was an adulterer, a liar, and a murderer. Nahum appears to be the angriest man who ever lived. Jonah was the rogue prophet who went east when

> **The reckless love of God for you is not found on just one page, but every page of the Bible.**

149

God told him to go west. The apostle Peter denied Jesus *three* times. James and John thought they should sit at the right and left hand of Jesus' throne in heaven per the request of their mother, who seemed to be living vicariously through them. The apostle Paul was a murderer of Christians before his conversion. In this short list alone, we see that three of the most popular men in the Bible—Moses, David, and Paul—had each killed someone.

This exhausting approach of looking for heroes to emulate results in malnourished disciples, because the aim is not feasting on the only meal Scripture offers: the person and work of Jesus. It's like opening a bag of potato chips that is 50 percent air, and even once you get into it, there's no real sustenance. At the end of the day, you will either be looking for heroes in the Bible and feel overwhelming pressure to become one yourself, or you will see Jesus as the true Hero of Scripture, who at the expense of his own life, saved yours.

The Whole Bible Is About Jesus

The ending of the gospel of Luke provides the key to seeing the overall purpose of Scripture as Jesus teaches the disciples on the evening of his resurrection.

> Then he said to them, "These are my words that I spoke to you while I was still with you, that everything written about me in the Law of Moses and the Prophets and the Psalms must be fulfilled." Then he opened their minds to understand the Scriptures, and said to them, "Thus it is written, that the Christ should suffer and on the third day rise from the dead, and that repentance and forgiveness of sins should

be proclaimed in his name to all nations, beginning from Jerusalem."

Luke 24:44–47

British theologian Christopher Wright says,

This text provides the hermeneutical compass for the way disciples of Jesus must read the Old Testament Scriptures, that is, both messianically and missiologically. . . . We can undoubtedly feel the pulse of that promise (the promise of God to bless the nations through Abraham) in these great phrases.[5]

Jesus says the entire Old Testament is about him, and we see that the New Testament apostles find their entire ministry rooted in Jesus. They preach the implications of who Christ is and what it means to know him, be loved by him, follow him, and make him known. Jesus is the point of the Old Testament, and repentance and forgiveness of sins should be proclaimed in his name to all nations. Nobody is exempt from extending the reckless love of God on display in the gospel and made personal through repentance of sin.

Jesus Is the Point of the Whole Bible

Unfortunately, it is possible to read the Bible and miss Jesus. I know, because I have done it. The ancient rabbis did this in the first century, and many do it today in the twenty-first century. In his gospel, John depicts Jesus debating with a group of popular Jewish leaders and their followers on the Sabbath. After healing on the Sabbath (which was a big no-no for this crowd) and making himself "equal with

God" (John 5:18), things became more heated. John records Jesus saying:

> You search the Scriptures because you think that in them you have eternal life; and it is they that bear witness about me, yet you refuse to come to me that you may have life. I do not receive glory from people. But I know that you do not have the love of God within you. I have come in my Father's name, and you do not receive me. If another comes in his own name, you will receive him. How can you believe, when you receive glory from one another and do not seek the glory that comes from the only God? Do not think that I will accuse you to the Father. There is one who accuses you: Moses, on whom you have set your hope. For if you believed Moses, you would believe me; for he wrote of me. But if you do not believe his writings, how will you believe my words?
>
> John 5:39–47

These men who doubted and accused Jesus had devoted their entire lives to mastering the Old Testament texts both in content and practice. They'd even invented rules to supplement the rules so as to make sure that the Bible's commands were kept. Yet here we have Jesus saying that their study of the Scriptures is in vain, all for nothing, complete hogwash! He declares that the Scriptures point to him, and his listeners can't stomach the thought of coming to him who appears to be mortal, a mere human being, for eternal life. Jesus elaborates by saying that Moses' words will stand in judgment over them because even Moses was doing more than giving laws to observe. Rather, he intentionally directed his followers and readers to Christ, who would save his people by grace through faith. Knowing what texts Jesus had in mind here is difficult.

However, Matthew, who writes to a very Jewish audience that was quite concerned with Jesus' relationship to the Old Testament, probably had a few in mind. In fact, when it comes time for him to write his gospel, he helpfully provides many texts as he repeatedly emphasizes Jesus' fulfillment of the Old Testament's promises and prophecies (see Matthew 1:22; 2:15; 4:14; 8:17; 12:17; 13:35; 17:23; 21:4; 26:56; and 27:9). Furthermore, in Luke 24, after Jesus is resurrected, he has a conversation both on the Emmaus road with Cleopas and an unnamed disciple, and then again while having breakfast with his disciples. Jesus makes this revolutionary statement:

> Then he said to them, "These are my words that I spoke to you while I was still with you, that everything written about me in the Law of Moses and the Prophets and the Psalms must be fulfilled." Then he opened their minds to understand the Scriptures.
>
> Luke 24:44–45

Consider the implications of these statements. Jesus says the whole Bible is about him. He is not asking us to hijack the text and force him into the pages of the Old Testament. As a Jew, he would never think of such a thing. Rather, he simply, humbly, and truthfully says in effect, "Look and see me there! No pressure necessary. You don't have to read me into the text. Merely read the text and I emerge." But even after we meet Jesus in the Bible and are converted, we are not finished with his book. Instead, our conversion marks the beginning of a lifetime of going deeper and deeper into the Word of God.

This Christ-centered way of reading the Bible has massive implications on both our discipleship and our mission as Christians, because the reckless love of God is at the blazing center of our identity and all that we do. Each text is given that we may be further conformed to the image of Jesus (see 2 Timothy 3:16–17; Romans 8:29). If we fail to see a text in terms of its being planted at the feet of Jesus and his mission for the world, we have missed the point. Soon the Bible is reduced to a list of do's and don'ts. Heroes and villains. Good guys and bad guys. Winners and losers. The good news of the gospel, when seen in this light, is reduced to good advice at best. And those who supposedly know Jesus will relate to him in such a manner that it's as if they don't know him. Like when Ned Flanders on *The Simpsons* told his boys, "Okay boys, when you meet Jesus, make sure you call him Mr. Christ."

> **The reckless love of God is at the blazing center of our identity and all that we do.**

Jesus didn't come to give good advice. He came to tell of the wrath to come and to call people to repentance, to extend the incomprehensible love of God to the world, to summon us to follow him no matter the cost, and to enter into joy unspeakable. Jesus did not come to be our homeboy or our life coach. He assumed the role of God. Westminster theologian and author Michael Horton says, "One can lose weight, stop smoking, improve one's marriage, and become a nicer person without Jesus."[6] In other words, when we understand the Bible to be a list of good guys and bad guys, it can easily become a self-help book rather than the revolutionary good news that changes hearts and turns lives upside down. Therefore, the Bible's purpose is most certainly not to divide us into teams of winners and losers, successes and failures. It plainly says that we are *all* bad guys, that Jesus is the only good guy, and that the Bible's purpose is to get us to him.

Brennan Manning, author of *The Ragamuffin Gospel* and *Abba's Child*, asks,

> How is it then that we've come to imagine that Christianity consists primarily in what we do for God? How has this come to be the good news of Jesus? Is the kingdom that he proclaimed to be nothing more than a community of men and women who go to church on Sunday, take an annual spiritual retreat, read their Bibles every now and then, vigorously oppose abortion, don't watch X-rated movies, never use vulgar language, smile a lot, hold doors open for people, root for their favorite team, and get along with everybody? Is that why Jesus went through the bleak and bloody horror of Calvary? Is that why He emerged in shattering glory from the tomb? Is that why He poured out his Holy Spirit on the Church? To make nicer men and women with better morals?[7]

Of course not. Resuscitation and resurrection are two different things. Human beings are dead in sin and in need of more than moral improvement; we need to be overcome by the love of God and transformed by his resurrecting power. Yes, *resurrection*. As the late Swiss Catholic theologian Hans Urs von Balthasar said,

> Of course, it would be meaningless to speak of the Cross without considering the other side, the Resurrection of the

Crucified. "If Christ has not risen, then our preaching is nothing and also your faith is nothing; you are still in your sins and also those who have fallen asleep . . . are lost. If we are merely people who have put their hope in Christ in this life, then we are the most pitiful of all men" (1 Cor. 15:14, 17–19). If one does away with the fact of the Resurrection, one also does away with the Cross, for both stand and fall together, and one would then have to find a new center for the whole message of the gospel. What would come to occupy this center is at best a mild father-god who is not affected by the terrible injustices in the world, or man in his immorality and hope who must take care of his own redemption: "atheism in Christianity."[8]

Jesus: The Hero of the Whole Bible

Sally Lloyd-Jones, author of the *The Jesus Storybook Bible*, tells children the Bible is more than a book of rules and more than a story of heroes and villains: "The Bible is most of all an adventure story about a young hero who comes from a far country to win back his lost treasure. It's a love story about a brave prince who leaves his palace, his throne—everything, to rescue the ones he loves. It's like the most wonderful of fairy tales that has come true in real life!"[9] Thus, Jesus is the hero because he is superior to everyone and everything in the Bible.

I am forever indebted to pastor Tim Keller, who opened my eyes to seeing the "true and better Jesus" throughout the Bible.[10] Jesus surpasses Adam, who rebelled, broke fellowship with God, and fell into temptation in the garden of Eden. Jesus remained obedient and did not fail his test in the garden of Gethsemane. He didn't hide from God his father, but prayed to him, totally submitting himself to his will, and thereby bringing restoration with God to sinners. Jesus transcends Abel, who was vengefully slain, but who sinned. Jesus remained a sinless sacrifice. Jesus is greater than Noah. While Noah built the ark to save people from the flood, Jesus became the Ark and absorbed the wrath of God so that all who enter him would be saved. Likewise, Jesus is greater than Abraham, who by faith offered his son Isaac as a sacrifice. Jesus became the perfect sacrifice. Jesus is greater than Isaac, who was asked to carry wood to the place of sacrifice. Jesus carried his wooden cross to Calvary.

Jesus exceeds Joseph, who, after suffering at his brothers' hands, was appointed to the right hand of the king of Egypt and then forgave and provided for his betrayers. Jesus sits at the right hand of God, extending grace and providing for us who have betrayed him. Jesus transcends Moses, who was a mediator between God and man while on earth and gave us the law as it was given to him. Jesus lives as our *only* mediator between God and man, who gave us the Law of the new covenant, his law of love—not written on stones but in his blood!

Jesus is greater than Job, for while Job served God well, he endured extreme suffering. Jesus suffered as a sinless man. And just as Job's friends failed him, Jesus' disciples failed him in his final hours. Jesus is greater than Esther, for unlike Esther, who risked her life by entering the palace before the king, Jesus freely gave his life at Pilate's palace. Jesus is greater than Boaz. When Boaz redeemed Ruth and brought her and her despised people into community with God's people, he foreshadowed what Jesus would do to redeem his bride—the church—from all the nations of the earth.

Though descended from King David's line, Jesus excels David. While David killed the giant Goliath, Jesus defeated Satan, sin, death, hell, and the wrath of God. Again, Jesus, rather than avoiding war like David, went to war to reclaim God's people. Rather that committing adultery like David, Jesus saved the prostitute and restored her dignity. Also, rather than covering sin as David did with both Bathsheba and Uriah, Jesus, the true light, exposes and forgives sin.

Jesus is greater than Elijah, who offered sacrifices at Mount Carmel. Instead, Jesus became the sacrifice—not to prove YHWH of Israel is the one true God, but to offer himself as YHWH's Son, who destroys the works of the devil. Jesus is greater than Jonah. While Jonah spent three days in the belly of the fish, thus eventually leading to the repentance of many in Nineveh, Jesus spent three days in the grave, which led to far greater salvation. And rather than pouting over those who repented, like Jonah did, Jesus and the angels rejoice when one lost sinner repents.

Jesus surpasses Nehemiah, who rebuilt Jerusalem, for Jesus ushers in the New Jerusalem. Jesus is greater than Hosea, who married a prostitute whom he continued to love even though she was an unfaithful wife. In a greater way, Jesus does even more for his unfaithful bride—the church. Jesus remains the true pillar of fire as he is the light of the world and leads his people. He is the greatest prophet, who proclaims the final and true word. Jesus is greater than the rock that was struck in the desert, as he unceasingly provides living water for everlasting life.

Jesus is the great High Priest who does not sacrifice animals but gave his own life as a sacrifice. He is the true King of all kings, who liberates and pays the citizens' debts. Jesus is the great Judge who restores his people. Jesus is the true temple of God that we enter to worship the LORD. Jesus is the final lamb that takes away the sins of the world. Jesus is the living bread come down from heaven, and as the Israelites were fed in the wilderness, Christians are sustained by Jesus' body. It's not hard to see why theologians speak so often of "redemptive history." History is redemptive because there is a redeemer! Therefore, when Jesus the Redeemer claims the Bible is *his* story, we must believe it.

Harvard professor emeritus Frank Moore Cross writes:

> Jesus did not propose to present a new system of universal truths. He came to fulfill the past work of God, to confirm the faith of the fathers, to open the meaning of the Law and Prophets. The New Testament does not set aside or supplant the Old Testament. It affirms it, and, from its point of view, completes it. Lines of continuity between Moses and Jesus, Isaiah and Jesus, the Righteous Teacher and Jesus, John the Baptist and Jesus should occasion no surprise. On the contrary, a biblical faith insists on such continuities. The biblical faith is not a system of ideas, but a history of God's acts of redemption.[11]

This true and better Jesus who is the point, the pinnacle, and the crown jewel of the entire Bible is extending not a contract but *covenantal love* to you in this very moment.

Reading the Bible Missionally

Not only does the Bible affect our discipleship and knowledge of Jesus, it also demands a missional posture that we should assume before the world. Based on his own words,

Jesus intends the Bible to be read, understood, and applied in specific ways. Upon one's encounter with the reckless love of God, Jesus intends that this message get out to the nations. Why talk about the Bible and mission? How do they relate? Here's how. Cambridge scholar Christopher Wright emphasizes that a text of the Bible "often has its origin in some issue, need, controversy, or threat that the people of God needed to address in their context of mission. The text itself is a product of mission in action."[12] Wright is saying that the Bible is a document, a product that is the result of men who observed and encountered God, who is on a mission to save the world through His Son and by His Spirit. Yes, the Bible records God's revelation to mankind (though not exhaustible)—God is revealed as perfect, glorious, just, and extending undeniable reckless love for people just like you. This profoundly changes not only how we view what the Bible is but also how we read it, understand it, and then respond to it. This is what makes the good news, *good news*. Good news is impossible to keep to oneself. It simply must be shared.

The prophet Jeremiah had an incredibly hard ministry and is commonly known as the "weeping prophet." His life was riddled with despair and heartache. In chapter 20 of his prophecy, he reflects on turning back, not going forth with the Word of God to the people, and then concludes that it is "in my heart as it were a burning fire shut up in my bones, and I am weary with holding it in, and I cannot" (Jeremiah 20:9). God confronts us with his Word, brings us to repent of our sins, which is a painful process for every one of us, heals us with his love, abides with us, and then *sends us* into the world with the reconciling message that God has come to wage war on sin, but loves, saves, and keeps those who were once considered his enemies. Thus, the Christian is tasked with studying, or exegeting, a few things.

Exegete a Few Things

The word *exegete* means to "lead out," "to exit," and "to extract from"—as in critical interpretation. Think "exodus." Christians who are on mission to see unbelievers see and savor the reckless love of God are constantly interpreting three things: Scripture, culture, and oneself. It could be said that the Christian who sets her focus on God's glory and others must constantly read, interpret, and respond not only to the Biblical text but also to these other "texts." This is getting down into the more earthy stuff known as contextualization—making sense out of God's Word to real people, in real space, in real time, right in front of them. For many today, the Bible is a dusty old book that nobody reads or takes seriously anymore, much less the radical love of God revealed therein. Therefore, part of loving our neighbor means that we thoughtfully seek to understand and engage in the world they currently live in and speak in a winsome and relevant way—not just assume that they should believe God loves them as they are but won't leave them the way they are.

> **Christians who are on mission to see unbelievers see and savor the reckless love of God are constantly interpreting three things: Scripture, culture, and oneself.**

Exegete the Scripture

So, when it comes to reading the Bible, we don't want to know just *what* the Bible is saying, but *why* is it there. Trying to understand the original context of a particular passage really matters. This is because a text isn't always completely up for grabs. The author had something to say right then, right there. Questions about authorship, recipients, and occasions for writing are all factors in how one interprets the text. Who wrote this? Moses? Solomon? Luke? Paul? Who was it written to? The nation of Israel? A pastor? A church? When was it written? During a battle, or a time of peace? Who was in political power? Pharaoh or Nero? What was the occasion for writing? In Corinth, there were issues of drunkenness, sexual immorality, and other things. In the ancient city of Thessalonica, questions of last things in the Bible and history arose. What genre does this text belong to? Is this law, prophets, wisdom literature, gospel, history, a letter, or apocalyptic literature? In what language was this originally written? Is this an allegory or parable? What kind of connotations or images would *this* particular word or idea used by the author elicit in the mind of the first readers?

The Christian faith is a talking faith. We have news, a real message that must be communicated. Christians share the gospel in how we care for, counsel, teach, discuss and write about the gospel message. Hans-Georg Gadamer, a nineteenth-century Bible scholar who specialized in interpreting Scripture, said something every Christian needs to hear: It's not only about talking, but about *listening*. He insisted that hermeneutics (the science of interpretation) goes way beyond what one says with his mouth to what one hears with his ears. "Hermeneutics is above all a practice, the art of understanding. . . . In it, what one has to exercise above all is the ear."[13] This takes time, patience, humility, and an insatiable curiosity.

Theologian Ernst Fuchs often asked, "What do we have to do at our desks to make the New Testament come alive?" On one hand, this is a good question for any Christian to ask. On the other, it must be said that the Bible is already "living and active" (Hebrews 4:12). The problem in many cases is not with the Bible or a person's study of it. If the Word of God is not living and active, penetrating and piercing to the person who reads it and shares it, not only is God dishonored, but those who listen to that person will quickly be able to discern that and not take the Scriptures seriously either. Merely sitting at a desk all day and studying Scripture will not enable others to see how alive the Bible is. Christians must get up, go out, and *engage* the world around them, asking the right questions and being in a constant state of learning and appropriating.

Exegete the Culture

A missional reading of the Bible leads to an exegesis of the culture as well. Why study someone's culture? Because people who go to church are only at church a couple of hours a week and then spend the rest of their time planted in the middle of the culture that doesn't go to church or read the Bible or pray or anything of that nature. The culture constantly bombards Christians with its particular values, directions, and influences. So who are the culture makers and shapers in your city? Who holds the political offices? Who are the athletes that everyone is looking to? What is in fashion in your city? Why do you think the trend is going that way? What music are people listening to? What concerts are they attending? What books and websites are they are reading? What do people in this culture do for fun? All of this matters to the Christian who is reading the Bible missionally, because she wants to know how her non-church culture understands the world, God, themselves, and their community. More than that, this kind of insight helps the believer both confront the culture and celebrate it. Christians also have to be able to confront the particular sins and idols of that culture and not merely talk about sin generically.

Once gripped by the reckless love of God and engagement with the culture, the Christian must remain in a humble posture so that she does not see herself as better than anyone else. What I mean is this: When we see a prostitute on a street corner, we should not judge her and write her off as someone who made some bad choices and should be doing better with her life. That is the opposite of the heart response of someone who has encountered God's love. Rather, we should see that person and think, *That is a woman who needs to know God doesn't use her the way the world does. He loves her, wants to heal her, restore her, and bring her back to her true identity as his daughter. She could even be leading a Bible study in our church!* When we see high school kids outside a movie theater smoking pot, we shouldn't think, *I wish those kids would just get their act together and quit hanging around here.* Instead, our thoughts (and prayer) should be, *God, those boys are far from you. They're looking for happiness in something of the earth rather than in you, the Creator. May they come to find their home in your love. Maybe someday they'll be off to their first semester of Bible college!*

Celebrating what is going on in your area is equally important. Studying the culture provides believers grounds for pointing out the wins and successes of the area, whether those pertain to new businesses that are opening or recent renovations to a local elementary school. This shows the culture that we're actually *present* and talking to them *right here and right now,* not just going on about what happened "back in Bible days." Paul himself quoted the poets and philosophers in Acts 17 for a reason. He loved his people more fully by immersing himself in their world, speaking their language. Striving to be "well thought of by outsiders" (1 Timothy 3:7) was not something he merely expected of other pastors. No, this was for him to practice too. He purposely used culture to connect with those he wanted to introduce to Jesus. Indeed, he was perceptive (Acts 17:16, 22). What do *you* perceive?

Exegete Self

Finally, Christians reading the Bible missionally must allow the Holy Spirit and the Scriptures to exegete them as well. Paul tells the Colossian Christians to "let the word of Christ *dwell* in you richly, teaching and admonishing one another in all wisdom, singing psalms and hymns and spiritual songs, with thankfulness in your hearts to God" (Colossians 3:16). The Word of Christ isn't just something that Christians read and share. The Word *reads us as well.* Jesus said, "Out of the abundance of the heart the mouth speaks" (Matthew 12:34).

How Christians encounter Jesus in the Scriptures can and will have the greatest impact when speaking to friends about the gospel. Whether or not all of one's exegesis is perfect (it won't be), since the beginning of the church, people have been able to recognize those who "have been with Jesus" (Acts 4:13). John Calvin said,

> It is evident that man never attains a true self-knowledge until he has previously contemplated the face of God, and come down after such contemplation to look into himself.[14]

A person who is effective in sharing the love of God with others knows his own sin and his own desperation for Jesus. As a result, he becomes even more burdened to better communicate grace and the need for Jesus to his people.

Beginning with the call of Abram and culminating in the new heaven and new earth, the Bible records and proclaims that we are far more sinful than we can imagine. But Jesus is a greater Savior than we could have ever hoped for, and through Jesus, we are spotless in God's eyes. To read the Bible and then conclude it means anything other than being deeply loved by God, conformed to the image of Jesus (Romans 8:29), and extending his message of repentance and belief in the gospel (Mark 1:14), simply misses the point of each book, sixty-six times in a row.

Conclusion

A Personal Relationship With Jesus?

My plea is simple and profound. I have one mission that is two-fold—to encourage Christians to take their ten-thousandth step of faith into a deeper, more authentic walk with Jesus. There's more than enough grace awaiting you in God's Word, in moments of prayer, in hours of service, and a lifetime in his community known as the church. The love of God is personal and passionate and is intended to be experienced. As John Calvin himself declared in his *Christian Institutes,*

> Doctrine is not a matter of talk but of life. It is not grasped by the intellect alone, like other branches of learning. It is received only when it fills the soul and finds a home in the inmost recesses of the heart.[1]

I also plead with nonbelievers to consider the broad historical shoulders upon which I stand to make these claims and to step out in faith toward an authentic, face-to-face encounter with the central figure of the Bible—Jesus Christ. He knows you better than anyone and has a ferocious, life-changing, sin-forgiving, guilt-removing, shame-destroying love for *you*.

So whether you have known Jesus for fifty years or whether he's calling you for the first time, the offer stands. He cannot be distracted from his late-night prayer at Gethsemane. Filled with unrivaled passion, his holy, perfect work cost him his life, and through this work, he takes away the sins you have committed while healing the pain of the sins committed against you. For all of this, he charges nothing. That is what grace is, my friend. *Accepting this truth allows you to be joyously shaped for the rest of your life.*

Reading through the pages of the New Testament, you'll notice Jesus isn't looking to your parents, grandparents, or anyone else in the church to exercise *your* unique faith in him. Martin Luther said, "Every man must do two things. He must do his own believing and his own dying." Looking to someone else to believe *for* you would trivialize Jesus' specific work on the cross for you as an individual. Second, it would negate everything said about the personal nature of the Holy Spirit, the third person of the Trinity.

Your Creator God uses only one mediator—Jesus Christ. Can you accept the fact that Jesus loves you right where you are, and that you can have confidence in his love and trust what is written in the Bible?

If you step forward, it won't be long before you ask questions that every other Christian has asked: *What if I don't see incredible changes right away? What if I don't get any better? What if sin still looks appealing? What if I forget to pray or say thank you? What if I don't feel like reading my Bible sometimes?* The answer to these questions and others is that this unchanging message of God's grace will empower all that it requires.

Put another way, God's commandments, sometimes known as *disciplines*, really aren't so much disciplines as *joys*. His love for you is not riding on anything you do or don't do. I've heard this aphorism: "If you'll just take one step toward God, he'll take the last ninety-nine to get to you." Actually, God takes all one hundred steps as he reconciles the lost to himself and then helps us to reconcile with one another. Consider that Jonah and the Ninevites, who repented at his preaching, reside in the same heaven, as well as Paul and the apostle Stephen, whose murder Paul condoned. Even Abraham, the man of faith, as well as the thief on the cross

Can you accept the fact that Jesus loves you right where you are, and that you can have confidence in his love and trust what is written in the Bible?

whom Jesus promised paradise, gather around the throne of God today by grace through faith. In fact, the fear of the law does not empower forward movement. It is accomplished by grace and grace alone.

The Tale of a Healthy Husband and a Sick Wife

Take a gloriously messy community, multiply it by millions, and we have the church. Today, giving up on the church is easy. I understand. As a pastor and teacher, hardly a day passes that I don't hear someone complain about the church. Yes, she's got a lot of problems and is sick much of the time. She sometimes yawns through worship and counts the lights when God's words of love to her are read. She looks at the floor when asked about her wedding day. She conveniently forgets to wear her wedding ring when old boyfriends come to town. Rather than etching love on her heart, she opts to have it screen-printed on coffee cups, T-shirts, bumper stickers, and bracelets. She thinks, *This will do, no need to go overboard*. She often slurs her speech when talking about the important things like creation, the cross, heaven, or hell. She's mocked, kicked, ridiculed, scoffed at, and bruised by the Academy, Hollywood, and the self-sufficient. Even more, she was prone to violence during the Crusades. Today, in the West, poor theology tells her only how wretched she is, that this world is a prison, and that Paradise *is* lost and will only be found by those who keep the rules perfectly.

Many days and in many places, she appears confused, wayward, stubborn, and afraid. She's unfaithful, and sometimes inconsiderate. She's often either too quick or too slow in all the wrong places. She's quick to open her mouth with ill-informed opinions and then clumsily passes judgment. In her immaturity, she'll cut in line because the way she sees it, no matter how many times she hears the opposite, "The first will be first and the last will be last." She's slow to listen to God and people and reluctant to welcome the far-off and forget about her origins. She's looking out for number one and no one else. Augustine is attributed with the painfully honest reflection that "the Church is a whore and she's our mother." If you're of the church, I'm describing you, and I'm also describing me more often than I'd care to admit.

But we need to be careful about how we talk about and treat the church. After all, this is Jesus' wife, and because she's married to Jesus, she won't always be this way. In fact, if you think she's difficult now, you should have seen her before she met Jesus. Yes, the Bible admonishes us to look beyond *that* guy or *that* girl, *that* pastor who let you down and *proved* to you that he really was human after all, and look to Jesus (Hebrews 12:2),who is the head of the church (Colossians 1:17).

> **We need to be careful about how we talk about and treat the church.**

There's more to celebrate about the church than to complain about. There's more to celebrate than to mourn. So refuse to slander her, and instead serve her, because Jesus does. You see, minute by minute, hour by hour, day by day, she's becoming more like her husband, one person at a time in both the smallest details, like her attitude at 7:45 in Monday morning traffic to the history-defining moments to be compared to nailing the Ninety-five Theses to the Wittenberg door (and starting the Reformation). And at the end of it all, we will see what John the apostle saw on the island of Patmos when the angel said to him, "Come, I will show you the Bride, the wife of the Lamb" (Revelation 21:9).

Jesus declares the church to be holy, and she is walking in the light. Jesus loves her, pursues her, is married to her, and gave his life for her. He woos her day after day and reminds her that he's building a home for her where they will live forever. He didn't accidentally end up in this "predicament" with her. He had options, and still chose her. That's part of what it means to be God. Having options. This is no high

171

school crush. That kind of silliness derogates his cross. This was his plan. He gave her his Spirit as a guarantee that his love is real and that she can trust all of his promises.

The writers of Scripture describe a coming day that is going to be the last day on God's calendar. On that day, we read that his bride, the church, will wear white, because she's cleaner than ever before. She will be presented to Jesus, sparkling, totally spotless, and the only four-letter word proceeding from her mouth will be "love."

Judges, prophets, priests, kings, apostles, and countless others throughout church history have given their lives to preserve this message that Jesus, God in the flesh, loves her (you) for the glory of God. Paul told the Roman Christians that they had received the pardoning grace of God and Jesus' righteousness, and that they should "not become proud, but fear" (Romans 11:20). Though not written directly to us, these first-century words are written *for* us today. You can see that the church is not the savior; Jesus is. Hence, that's what the *solas* were all about. Grace alone, faith alone, the Word alone, Christ alone, for the Glory of God alone.

Let me repeat that this is not a license for Christians to isolate ourselves in our personal relationship with Jesus and be part of a pseudo, self-absorbed, naval-gazing religion. Rather, Jesus loves you and me as individuals and wants an individual relationship with each of us via the Holy Spirit. But that's not all that I'm saying. Jesus isn't looking for lone ranger Christian heroes. That will land us flat on our faces. He knows we need his church and his community, and believe it or not, we need each other. If one person believes "Jesus loves me" and another person believes "Jesus loves me," that means we have "*Jesus loves us.*" The reckless love of God belongs to us! That *us* is the church. And we can't forget that *before* Christ, our lives weren't neat and tidy. We are still a work in progress, so we shouldn't be surprised when we meet someone who is struggling that they appear inconsiderate or rude. Encountering another work in progress isn't always neat, tidy, and simple.

We are intended to be conduits through which Jesus pours his love into this world.

Jesus loving you, and me, and us (the church) ought to have an absolutely profound impact on how we love one another. We are not simply silos that Jesus pours his love into. We are intended to be conduits *through which* Jesus pours his love into this world. You and I are to be like sponges. We soak up the love of Jesus and are to be wrung out in the church, loving one another.

Your church can have everything "right" and yet still get a rebuke from Jesus if love is absent. Take for example the church at Ephesus. In Revelation 2:2–3, Jesus says,

> I know your works, your toil and your patient endurance, and how you cannot bear with those who are evil, but have tested those who call themselves apostles and are not, and found them to be false. I know you are enduring patiently and bearing up for my name's sake, and you have not grown weary.

Can you imagine having a church like this? A community that works diligently and endures patiently, that doesn't tolerate evildoing, that tests those who are seeking to teach, so as to ensure sound doctrine, and that goes about doing all of this for the sake of Jesus, not themselves? However, Jesus says something that shows just how serious he is about love:

> But I have this against you, that you have abandoned the love you had at first. Remember therefore from where you have fallen; repent, and do the works you did at first. If not, I will come to you and remove your lampstand from its place, unless you repent.
>
> vv. 4–5

Some have read verse 4, "You have left your first love" (NASB) and interpreted it to mean "You have left me, Jesus, your first love." But that's not the intent based on what Jesus said prior, that he knows they are "enduring patiently and bearing up for [his] name's sake." They haven't left Jesus. So what does it say? "You have abandoned the love you had at first," meaning they were going about, serving in the body, without manifesting the love of Christ. Jesus cares not only about his love being seen clearly in the cross of his death and his resurrection, but that his gut-wrenching compassion, his all-encompassing grace be felt and dispersed in the church through the members of the church—you and me!

A Word to Mature Christians

If you have been a Christian for years and practically memorized the Twenty-third Psalm, John 3:16, and the Romans Road before you could walk, be encouraged that God, in his grace, found you when he did! Think back to when and where he introduced himself to you. Open up those passages one more time. There's more in them for you. Like the Author who wrote it, the Word is inexhaustible. King David wrote about "deep calling to deep." The bottomless cries from your soul and the riches of his Word correspond. There is more love to be received, more truth to be believed, and more good news to be savored among the "insiders" and shared with the "outsiders." Don't buy the lie that pushes you toward the lazy cop-outs that rob you from time with him and discipling others in his name.

A Word to New Christians: The Weekend Pace

For those who over the course of reading this book became a Christian or recently became a Christian, consider the Easter weekend. During Easter, Christians observe Good Friday, which marks the day Jesus gave his life, in our place, for our sins. Easter Sunday marks the day he rose from the grave, defeating sin, Satan, demons, and God's wrath. Strive to keep the Easter weekend first in your mind. The Christian life is not to be lived only in the shadow of Good Friday, mourning your sins, counting the losses, and trembling in the shame of sin. There is also resurrection Sunday's bursting light that brings us hope, security, and promise of new life! It's easy to get stuck on either Friday or Sunday. Some Christians you'll meet along the way will only sing a dirge of Good Friday and seem to have forgotten that Sunday is just around the bend. There are others who live only in resurrection Sunday, skipping about and acting as though sin didn't cause the death of God's Son. They tend to strike up the band only to drown out the world's sorrows. The reality of the Christian faith paces back and forth between Good Friday and Easter

Sunday, reminding us of who we were apart from Christ and where we were headed while simultaneously bursting with joy that we are forgiven, will wear white on the last day, and that suffering, sin, and pain in this world will expire.

As you sit down and open up your Bible, it can be quite intimidating. Here's where you start—invite the Author of the book to join you. His name is the Holy Spirit. The Bible is the only book in the world where the Author is always present with every reader, in any given language at any given time. Feel free to invite him to help you understand and apply his words to your life.

A Word on Conviction and Condemnation

In addition to this balancing of Good Friday and Easter Sunday, we need to know how to handle questions like *What do I do when I sin after becoming a Christian?* and *What is it that I'm feeling when I sin?* The Bible tells us that God hates sin. Because he wants us to walk in his joy and holiness, the Holy Spirit will convict us of sin. This conviction is constructive, not destructive. He's out to destroy *sin* in you, but not *you*.

However, God is not the only one who is at work. Paul tells us that our battle isn't with flesh and blood, but against rulers and authorities and powers (Ephesians 6:12). He also tells us that there is "no condemnation for those who are in Christ Jesus" (Romans 8:1). Satan, critics, and our flesh will condemn us. They will expect what is both impossible and unbiblical. These enemies don't ever go away. They may have seasons of greater or lesser accusations, but they will be around until Jesus finally crushes them under his feet.

Condemnation is a damning, destructive, soul-depleting experience. Its purpose is to cripple, not rehabilitate. So in the wake of sin, and as you are wrestling with the aftermath, ask yourself a couple of questions:

Why am I disturbed? King David asked this question often of his own soul (Psalm 42:5, 11; 43:5). Ask yourself: *Is what I'm experiencing right now going to lead me to holiness, repentance, and life with God or simply more sin and isolation? Are the steps that I'm going to walk in going to give God glory and bring me joy in him and to others?*

> **Jesus stood in your place condemned, that you might go free.**

How you answer these questions will let you know what to do next. If you're convicted by the Holy Spirit over sin, recall that "If we confess our sins, he [Jesus] is faithful and just to forgive our sins and to cleanse us from all unrighteousness" (1 John 1:9), and then move on. But if you're feeling condemned, simply remind yourself of what the Bible says about you—that you are loved, forgiven, blameless in God's eyes, and you ground your identity there. Recognize that you ought to be condemned for your sin, but that's not the whole story. Jesus stood in your place condemned, that you might go free. After all, whoever the Son sets free is "free indeed" (John 8:36).

A Word to Unbelievers

To you, the unbeliever, I must tell the truth. Anything other than the truth would be unloving. So here goes: Outside of

Jesus, you are headed toward eternal destruction in a place Jesus called hell. It is real, and it is where you will endure God's wrath forever because of your willful rebellion against his holy commands. You will not go to hell simply for rejecting the gospel message alone. Rather, your rejection of this message is simply what will be the final death blow, the coup de grace that seals your fate forever. You are under God's just condemnation. Your pardon does not come through trying harder to be a better person. Your pardon is through Jesus, who was wounded for our transgressions and stands victorious.

The good news is Jesus welcomes you warmly today to come to him, to trust him, and to receive his forgiveness. He longs for you to be filled with the Holy Spirit, to walk in new power all the way into your eternal home with him in heaven. Amid all of this, he invites you to revel in the fact that nothing can or will separate you from his love.

Such love transcends the greatest earthly love you can imagine. Such love has no strings attached; it is absolute grace poured out to you through Jesus' broken body and his shed blood. Such love does not make this world a candy store, for Jesus is not Santa Claus. But such love brings joy unspeakable and provides a foretaste of those eternal joys that God has prepared for those who love him and who claim the new life Jesus came to earth to bring.

Acknowledgments

I would like to acknowledge family and friends who have continued to encourage me and press me over the last few years.

First, my wife, Jana. Your AOL screen name from ages ago was "Agape412." I like to think God used that as a sign to say, "You'll be talking about my agape love for a long time." I fell in love with you the first time I laid eyes on you across a mosh pit at the age of nineteen, and I'm still on fire. You brighten, sweeten, and intensify everything about me. I want to be like you. May we remain discontent to merely warm ourselves by the fire of God's love and let us step into the fire and be utterly consumed. I am yours. You are mine. I love you.

To my mother, Beverly. I've seen the love of God in and through your life unlike anyone else. I am forever grateful to have the honor of calling you "Momma-nini." Nobody has cheered me on quite like you. Oh, and guess what? "I'm soooooo full!"

To my brother, Ernie. No, I didn't use your birth name here. I've never called you by your actual name. I never will.

You and I are ragamuffins to the end. I love you. Thank you for always being in my corner. I have countless favorite memories bound up with you and Dad: skipping church, eating Mexican pizzas, and watching pro wrestling, *The Simpsons*, and *Malcolm in the Middle*. Tag team partners forever!

To Papa Walt and Mrs. Sharon Sellers for their constant love, grace, and affection poured out on my family. Words just flat run out sometimes, don't they? In particular, the fiery-pistol Sharon helped edit the first draft of this book a few years ago and would meet with me to offer so much helpful insight and critique. On one occasion she told me, "Son, if you don't learn how to use a comma and a semicolon and start indenting, I'm gonna tan your hide ten ways to Sunday!" (I still don't know what that means exactly, but I sure believe that she was serious.) I consider y'all family. This means you're stuck with this fella.

Leonce Crump, my long-lost brother. Good grief. I don't know anyone I'd rather fight with or party with in the whole world. Thank you for standing for truth, justice, and the love of God the way you do. Thank you for consistently reminding me of who I am. Daddy D'z or Fox Bros. Bar-B-Q? Only we know who the real winner is. We are the definition of a feral cat family.

Brennan Manning. I don't know a writer or preacher who has influenced me more. How I look forward to meeting you in Abba's heaven one day.

The Acts 29 Network. I love these brothers. The friendships run deep. The brotherhood is real. To be in this with you men is life-giving to me. I sincerely love and respect you and your wives. Thank you for giving your lives to the thing Jesus gave his life for, the local church.

Notes

Introduction

1. John Calvin, *Institutes of the Christian Religion*, trans. Henry Beveridge, eds. Tony Lane and Hilary Osborne (1986; repr., Grand Rapids, MI: Baker Academic, 1987), 3:6.4, 161, 1987.

2. Paul Tillich, *The Courage to Be* (New Haven, CT: Yale University Press, 2000), 165.

3. Trevin Wax, "Gospel Definitions," June 2011, at http://trevinwax.com/wp-content/uploads/2009/09/Gospel-Definitions2.pdf.

4. Calvin, *Institutes*, 3:6.4.

5. J.I. Packer writes, "The Christian mainstream has construed impassibility as meaning not that God is a stranger to joy and delight, but rather that his joy is permanent, clouded by no involuntary pain," in *New Dictionary of Theology*, David Wright, Sinclair Ferguson, and J.I. Packer, eds. (Downers Grove, IL: InterVarsity, 1998), 277.

6. Jürgen Moltmann, *The Crucified God*, trans. John Bowdon and R. A. Wilson (Minneapolis: Augsburg Fortress, 1972), 222.

7. James Tomberlin and Peter van Inwagen, eds., *Alvin Plantinga* (Dordrecht: Reidel, 1985), 36.

8. Krish Kandiah, *Paradoxology* (London: Hodder & Stoughton, 2014), 64.

9. R. Laird Harris, Gleason L. Archer Jr., and Bruce K. Waltke, eds., *Theological Wordbook of the Old Testament* (Chicago: Moody, 1999).

10. Carmen Butcher, *The Cloud of Unknowing: With the Book of Privy Counsel* (Boston: Shambhala, 2009), 56–57.

11. Martin Luther, *A Commentary on Saint Paul's Epistle to the Galatians*, translated by Erasmus Middleton (Middletown, NY: Robert Carter and Brothers, 1854), 285.

Chapter 1: Jesus

1. Robert Kysar, *John, The Maverick Gospel*, 3rd ed. (Louisville, KY: Westminster John Knox, 2007), 60.

2. An oft-quoted saying attributed to H. G. Wells.

3. Kevin Vanhoozer, *Is There a Meaning in This Text?* (Grand Rapids, MI: Zondervan, 2009), 233.

4. Thomas Thompson and Thomas Verenna, eds., introduction to *Is This Not the Carpenter?: The Question of the Historicity of the Figure of Jesus* (Sheffield: Equinox, 2012). Quoted in Neil Godfrey, "Is This Not the Carpenter? The Question of the Historicity of the Figure of Jesus," December 23, 2010, http://vridar .wordpress.com/2010/12/23/is-this-not-the-carpenter-a-question-of-historicity/.

5. C. S. Lewis, *Mere Christianity* (New York: HarperOne, 1980), 52.

6. Hans-Georg Gadamer, "Reflections on My Philosophical Journey," in *The Philosophy of Hans-Georg Gadamer*, ed. Lewis E. Hahn (Chicago: Open Court, 1997), 3–63. Quoted in Anthony Thiselton, *Hermeneutics: An Introduction* (Grand Rapids, MI: Eerdmans, 2009), 2.

7. Charles Kraft, *Christianity in Culture* (Maryknoll, NY: Orbis Books, 2005), 175.

8. Brennan Manning, *The Furious Longing of God* (Colorado Springs: David C. Cook, 2009), 38.

Chapter 2: Loves

1. Aldous Huxley, *Complete Essays*, ed. Robert S. Baker (Chicago: I. R. Dee, 2002), 5:229.

2. Dietrich Bonhoeffer, *The Cost of Discipleship* (New York: Touchstone, 1959), 304.

3. Matthew Elliott, *Faithful Feelings* (Grand Rapids, MI: Kregel, 2006), 153.

4. Brad Young, *Jesus the Jewish Theologian* (Grand Rapids, MI: Baker Academic, 1995), 238, emphasis added.

5. Brennan Manning, *Lion and Lamb* (Grand Rapids, MI: Revell, 2004), 127.

6. Henri Nouwen, Donald McNeill, and Douglas Morrison, *Compassion* (New York: Doubleday, 1983), 24.

7. W. A. Elwell and P. W. Comfort, *Tyndale Bible Dictionary* (Wheaton, IL: Tyndale House, 2001), 306.

8. Flavius Josephus, *Antiquities of the Jews* 3:264.

9. Herman Strack and Paul Billerbeck, *Kommentar* (Munich: Beck, 1965), 4/2:750–51; on leprosy in general see 4/2:743–63. Quoted in James R. Edwards, *Is Jesus the Only Savior?* (Grand Rapids, MI: Eerdmans, 2005), 84.

10. B.B. Warfield, *The Emotional Life of Our Lord* (1912), Kindle edition.

11. Brother Lawrence, *The Practice of the Presence of God* (Rockville, MD: Wildside, 2010), 114.

12. For a discussion of sociological background in the ancient world, see B. Malina, *Christian Origins and Cultural Anthropology* (Atlanta: John Knox, 1986). For a discussion of honor and shame, see also Malina, *The Gospel of John in Sociolinguistic Perspectives* (Berkeley, CA: Center for Hermeneutical Studies

in Hellenistic and Modern Culture, 1985); Malina, *The New Testament World* (Atlanta: John Knox, 1981), esp. 25–50.

Chapter 3: Me (Part 1)

1. Lesslie Newbigin, *Missionary Theologian: A Reader* (London: SPCK, 2006), 27.

2. Sally Lloyd-Jones, *The Jesus Storybook Bible* (Grand Rapids, MI: Zondervan, 2007).

3. Fred Rogers, *The World According to Mister Rogers* (New York: Hyperion, 2003), 25.

Chapter 4: Me (Part 2)

1. Leonard Cohen, "Anthem," *The Future*, Sony/ATV Music Publishing Company, 1992.

2. Some speculate the immediate forgiveness of sins because paralysis can be one of the symptoms of having syphilis. Thus the man could have been paralyzed due to sexual immorality.

3. F.F. Bruce, *The Gospel of John* (Grand Rapids, MI: Eerdmans, 1983), 246.

Chapter 5: Me (Part 3)

1. Charles Spurgeon, "Beloved, and Yet Afflicted" (sermon, Mentone, France, 1518), http://www.spurgeon.org/sermons/1518.htm.

2. John R.W. Stott, *Christian Basics: A Handbook of Beginnings, Beliefs and Behaviour* (Downers Grove, IL: InterVarsity, 1992), 21.

3. Paul Tillich, *The Courage to Be* (New Haven, CT: Yale University Press, 2000), 170.

4. See Sylvia Wilkey Collinson, *Making Disciples: The Significance of Jesus' Educational Methods for Today's Church* (Carlisle: Paternoster, 2004), 11–26. See also K. H. Rengstorf, "Mathetes," *Theological Dictionary of the New Testament* 4:446–50; M. Hengel, *The Charismatic Leader and His Followers*, trans. J. Greig (Edinburgh: T&T Clark, 1981), 50–51.

5. Paul W. Barnett, *Jesus and the Logic of History* (Downers Grove, IL: InterVarsity, 1997), 140.

6. Flavius Josephus, *The War of the Jews* 2.640–41.

7. Ched Myers, *Binding the Strong Man: A Political Reading of Mark's Story of Jesus* (Maryknoll, NY: Orbis Books, 2008), 132.

8. James R. Edwards, *The Gospel According to Mark* (Grand Rapids, MI: Eerdmans, 2002), 49. See also Mendel Nun, *The Sea of Galilee and Its Fishermen in the New Testament* (Kibbutz Ein Gev: Kinnereth Sailing Company, 1989), 23–27; and Morna D. Hooker, *The Gospel According to Saint Mark* (Grand Rapids, MI: Baker Academic, 1991), 60.

9. Brett McKay, "Of Men and Nicknames," *The Art of Manliness*, September 24, 2012, http://artofmanliness.com/2012/09/24/of-men-and-nicknames/.

10. Walker Percy, *The Moviegoer* (New York: Random House, 1998), 193.

11. Michael Card, *Luke: The Gospel of Amazement* (Downers Grove, IL: InterVarsity, 2010), 247.

12. Ibid.

13. Corpus Christanorum, series Latina (Turnhout, Belgium: Brepols, 1953), CCL 77:261–62.

14. Richard Selzer, *Mortal Lessons: Notes on the Art of Surgery* (New York: Houghton Mifflin, 1996), 24.

15. Fil Anderson, *Breaking the Rules: Trading Performance for Intimacy with God* (Downers Grove, IL: InterVarsity, 2010), 205.

16. Thrice, "Words in the Water," *Major/Minor*, Vagrant Records, 2011.

17. Selzer, *Mortal Lessons*, 46.

18. Brennan Manning, *The Furious Longing of God* (Colorado Springs: David C. Cook, 2009), 31.

19. R.T. France, *The Gospel of Matthew* (Grand Rapids, MI: Eerdmans, 2007), 964, emphasis added.

20. Quoted in Paul D. Janz, *The Command of Grace: A New Theological Apologetics* (New York: T&T Clark, 2009), 69.

Chapter 6: This I Know

1. Richard Baxter, *The British Flac and Christian Sentinel* (Trafalgar's Square: Army Scripture Readers and Soldiers' Friend Society, 1878), 147.

2. G.K. Chesterton, *Orthodoxy* (India: Feather Trail Press, 2009), 14.

3. Anne Lamott, *Bird by Bird: Some Instructions on Writing and Life* (New York: Anchor Books, 1995), 22.

4. John Newton, "Amazing Grace," stanza two, public domain.

5. Andrew Brower Latz, "A Short Note Toward a Theology of Abiding in John's Gospel," *Journal of Theological Interpretation* 4, no. 2 (2010): 163.

6. Blaise Pascal, *Pensées* (New York: Dutton, 1958), 58.

7. Hans Kung, *On Being a Christian* (New York: Doubleday, 1984), 271.

8. Martin Luther, *What Luther Says: An Anthology*, ed. Ewald M. Plass (St. Louis: Concordia Publishing House, 1959), 2:704, no. 5.

9. Anthony C. Thiselton, *Two Horizons: New Testament Hermeneutics and Philosophical Description* (Grand Rapids, MI: Eerdmans, 1993), 269.

10. Joanne Carlson Brown and Rebecca Parker, "For God So Loved the World?" in *Christianity, Patriarchy, and Abuse: A Feminist Critique*, eds. Joanne Carlson Brown and Carole R. Bohn (New York: Pilgrim), 26.

11. Daniel McCullough, *Waking from the American Dream: Growing Through Your Disappointments* (Downers Grove, IL: InterVarsity, 1988), 91.

12. Nigel Wright, *A Theology of the Dark Side: Putting the Power of Evil in Its Place* (Eugene, OR: Wipf & Stock, 2010), 186.

13. Karl Barth, *Church Dogmatics* (Louisville: Westminster John Knox, 1994), 4/1, 59.2.

14. B. B. Warfield, "On The Emotional Life of Our Lord," in *Biblical and Theological Studies* (New York: Scribner's Sons, 1912), 77.

15. Donald Guthrie, *New Testament Theology* (Downers Grove, IL: Inter-Varsity, 1981), 454.
16. Richard Bauckham, *The Bible in Politics: How to Read the Bible Politically* (London: SPCK, 2010), 148, emphasis added.
17. R. C. Sproul, *What Is Reformed Theology? Understanding the Basics* (Grand Rapids, MI: Baker Books, 2005), 68.
18. Thomas R. Schreiner, *Galatians* (Grand Rapids, MI: Zondervan, 2010), 173.

Chapter 7: The Bible Tells Me So

1. George Eldon Ladd, "The Search for Perspective," *Interpretation* 25 (1971): 56–57.
2. Amy Orr-Ewing, "Postmodern Challenges to the Bible," in Ravi Zacharias, *Beyond Opinion: Living the Faith We Defend* (Nashville: Thomas Nelson, 2007), 3.
3. Stephen Prothero, *American Jesus: How the Son of God Became a National Icon* (New York: Farrar, Straus & Giroux, 2003), 11.
4. Everett Ferguson, *Backgrounds of Early Christianity*, 3rd ed. (Grand Rapids, MI: Eerdmans, 2003), 620.
5. Christopher Wright, *The Mission of God: Unlocking the Bible's Grand Narrative* (Downers Grove, IL: InterVarsity, 2006), 47.
6. Michael Horton, *Christless Christianity: The Alternative Gospel of the American Church* (Grand Rapids, MI: Baker Books, 2008), 102.
7. Brennan Manning, *The Furious Longing of God* (Colorado Springs: David C. Cook, 2009), 125.
8. Hans Urs von Balthasar, *A Short Primer for Unsettled Laymen* (San Francisco: Ignatius Press, 1985), 87.
9. Sally Lloyd-Jones, *The Jesus Storybook Bible: Every Story Whispers His Name* (Nashville: Thomas Nelson, 2007), 17.
10. Tim Keller, "Christ-Centered Ministry," https://vimeo.com/23642755.
11. Frank Moore Cross, *The Ancient Library of Qumran*, 3rd ed. (Sheffield: Sheffield Academic Press, 1995), 194.
12. Wright, *The Mission of God*, 49.
13. Hans-Georg Gadamer, "Reflections on My Philosophical Journey," in *The Philosophy of Hans-Georg Gadamer*, ed. Lewis E. Hahn (Chicago: Open Court, 1997), 3–63. Quoted in Anthony Thiselton, *Hermeneutics: An Introduction* (Grand Rapids, MI: Eerdmans, 2009), 2.
14. Calvin, *Institutes*, 1.38.

Conclusion

1. Calvin, *Institutes*, 3:6.4.

Alex Early (MDiv, New Orleans Baptist Theological Seminary; MA, London School of Theology) is a pastor who has planted a church in a bar, served as a theology professor, created the Acts 29 West Academy, a missional-theological training center, and launched the Acts 29 podcast. Alex lives with his wife and children in Atlanta, Georgia. He spends his downtime cooking with and for friends and family, and is pursuing a Doctor of Intercultural Studies degree at Western Seminary. Learn more at www.alxegesis.com.